The Brandon Guide for

Revise with **CLUESS** (pronounce as "clues" for easy memorization).

Coherence: Establish clear links between ideas. Use words such as *However, Otherwise, Therefore, Similarly, Hence, On the other hand, Then, Consequently, Also, Thus*. pp. 23, 33–34, 98, 124, 185

Language: Use words that fit your purpose and audience. Avoid slang, clichés, and vague words and phrases. pp. 23, 78–83, 204–205

Unity: Stay on your topic. Use strong topic sentences and theses. pp. 12–16, 23, 33–34

Emphasis: Call attention to important ideas. Repeat key words and phrases, often placing them near the beginning or end of a sentence, paragraph, or essay. pp. 4, 6, 23, 32–34, 80, 124

Support: Back up your controlling idea with evidence and logic. pp. 3–4, 7, 15–16, 21–32, 35, 57–58, 88–90, 171–172

Sentences: Write correct, effective sentences with structural variety. pp. 183–191

Edit with **CGPS** (pronounce as "see GPS" for easy memorization).

Capitalization: pp. 210–212

Grammar: pp. 182–205

Punctuation: pp. 205–210

Spelling: pp. 212–218

Brandon Writing Process Worksheet

Title _____

Name _____ **Due Date** _____

Assignment
(Use separate
paper if
needed.)

In the space below, write whatever you need to know about your assignment, including information about the topic, audience, pattern of writing, length, whether to include a rough draft or revised drafts, and whether your paper must be typed.

Stage One

Explore Freewrite, list, cluster, or take notes as directed by your instructor.

Stage Two

Organize Write a topic sentence or thesis; label the subject and focus parts.

Write an outline or an outline alternative. For reading-based writing, include references and short quotations with page numbers as support in the outline.

Stage Three
(Check off the
ten parts of
CLUESS and
CGPS as you
complete revis-
ing and editing.)

Write On separate paper, write and then revise your paragraph or essay as many times as necessary for coherence □, language (usage, tone, and diction) □, unity □, emphasis □, support □, and sentences □ (**CLUESS**). **Edit** problems in fundamentals, such as capitalization □, grammar □, punctuation □, and spelling □ (**CGPS**). **Read** your work aloud to hear and correct any structural errors or awkward-sounding sentences.

A-2

~ At a Glance

Writing Paragraphs and Beyond with Integrated Readings

SIXTH EDITION

Lee Brandon
Mt. San Antonio College

Kelly Brandon
Santa Ana College

CENGAGE
Learning

Australia • Brazil • Mexico • Singapore • United Kingdom • United States

CENGAGE
Learning®

At a Glance: Writing Paragraphs and Beyond with Integrated Readings, Sixth Edition

Lee Brandon and Kelly Brandon

Product Director: Annie Todd

Managing Developer: Megan Garvey

Development Editor: Margaret Manos

Content Coordinator: Elizabeth Rice

Product Assistant: Luria Rittenberg

Marketing Brand Manager: Lydia LeStar

Senior Content Project Manager: Aimee Chevrette Bear

Art Director: Faith Brosnan

Manufacturing Planner: Betsy Donaghey

Rights Acquisition Specialist: Ann Hoffman

Production Service: Books By Design, Inc.

Cover Designer: Walter Kopec, Boston

Cover Image: daitoZen/Flickr/Getty Images

Compositor: S4Carlisle Publishing Services

For product information and technology assistance, contact us at **Cengage Learning Customer & Sales Support, 1-800-354-9706**

For permission to use material from this text or product, submit all requests online at **www.cengage.com/permissions**. Further permissions questions can be emailed to **permissionrequest@cengage.com**.

Library of Congress Control Number: 2013948991

ISBN-13: 978-1-285-44468-0

ISBN-10: 1-285-44468-X

Cengage Learning
200 First Stamford Place, 4th Floor
Stamford, CT 06902
USA

Cengage Learning is a leading provider of customized learning solutions with office locations around the globe, including Singapore, the United Kingdom, Australia, Mexico, Brazil and Japan. Locate your local office at **international.cengage.com/region**.

Cengage Learning products are represented in Canada by Nelson Education, Ltd.

For your course and learning solutions, visit **www.cengage.com**.

Purchase any of our products at your local college store or at our preferred online store **www.cengagebrain.com**.

Instructors: Please visit **login.cengage.com** and log in to access instructor-specific resources.

Printed in the United States of America
2 3 4 5 6 7 17 16 15 14

Contents

12   Classification: Establishing Groups   134

13   Comparison and Contrast: Showing Similarities and Differences   144

16   Handbook   182

Preface

Performing for the Sixth Edition of *At a Glance: Writing Paragraphs and Beyond with Integrated Readings*, the surf writer, gallantly perched on a pencil, once more celebrates the "flow of writing." Like waves at a beach, writing is cyclical, moving forward and backward and forward again. As the students' guide and muse, the surf writer will always be searching for the "perfect wave," meaning the best possible written expression—one that is correct and effective. The recursive maneuvers of prewriting, organization, writing, revising and editing are the essence of that relentless search. Instructional dimensions of this book—comprehensive, flexible, relevant, and stimulating—are predicated on that systematic, relentless process.

Four Special New and Enhanced Features in the Sixth Edition

Feature One: New! The Brandon Guide for Revising and Editing

Just inside the front cover, you will see the **Self-Evaluation Chart for the Brandon Guide** for students to use in recording problems and progress in revising and editing.

On page A-1, the facing page, you will see a list of elements of the **Brandon Guide for Revising and Editing** in the form of acronyms. **CLUESS** (pronounced "clues") represents **C**oherence, **L**anguage, **U**nity, **E**mphasis, **S**upport, and **S**entences for revision. **CGPS** (pronounced "see GPS") represents **C**apitalization, **G**rammar, **P**unctuation, and **S**pelling for editing. All elements are keyed with page numbers to instruction in this book.

The Brandon Guide for Revising and Editing has several functions: It helps students organize and write their paragraphs and essays, provides a framework for cooperative assignments, and offers features of good writing that can be used (with appropriate modifications) for instructor-student conferences, peer-editing,

classroom instruction, and, perhaps—with even more modification—
department standards for placement or exit testing. Go online to
www.cengagebrain.com to download an enlarged copy of the Self-
Evaluation Chart for the Brandon Guide.

Feature Two: Enhanced! The Brandon Writing Process Worksheet (now with checkbox refinements)

Correlated with the Brandon Guide for Revising and Editing, the
Brandon Writing Process Worksheet (page A-2) provides a writing
guide for the student; it can also become a document showing the
development of the assignment for the instructor. It includes the
three stages of the writing process: **Explore** the topic (freewrite,
brainstorm, list, cluster, or take notes). **Organize** the content of
the proposed assignment by a topic outline beginning with a thesis. **Write** and revise the paragraph or essay as many times as
necessary for CLUESS, and edit it with CGPS. The worksheet can
be copied from page A-2 or downloaded in an enlarged form from
the Student Companion Site. The Instructor Companion Site also
provides a Word copy that can be customized by the Instructor
to fit a specific pedagogy or a particular assignment. Go online
to *www.cengagebrain.com* to download an enlarged copy of the
Brandon Writing Process Worksheet.

Feature Three: Enhanced! Reading-Based Writing

Reading-Based Writing Defined

Introduced in Chapters 4 and 5, and continued with applications
to readings in Chapters 6–15, the optional reading-based writing requires students to read a source, write an analytical reply, and give
credit to the source(s) for the ideas they borrow and the words they
quote. Credit can be noted formally (MLA in this book—or with APA
form, as presented on both the Student and the Instructor Companion Sites) or informally (by using clear references with acknowledged
credit and quotations with quotation marks), depending on the instructor's preference. As for structure, reading-based writing can be
a summary, a reaction (paragraph or essay), or a two-part response
(with separated summary and reaction). Although the reaction can
include personal experience to clarify and support conclusions, the
ideas from the readings should be at the focus of the topic sentence
or thesis. The reaction can also incorporate summary to convey a

broad aspect of the text. But summary is never the major concern of the reaction. Students who work with reading-based writing will be able to function better in writing across the curriculum and move more smoothly into advanced courses.

Reading-Based Writing in the Syllabus

Instructors who wish to help students transition from personal experience to more analytical thought with reading-based writing have choices that include: (1) beginning with the personal narrative and phasing in reading-based writing; (2) interspersing reading-based writing with other assignments; or (3) using reading-based writing throughout the course.

～ Other New, Refined, and Enhanced Material

- The **new** Chapter 4 on reading techniques for critical thinking and documented writing
- The **new** Chapter 12 (a returning feature) on writing paragraphs of classification
- 60 percent **new** reading selections (15 new to this edition)
- Now with 21 third-person readings
- Additional **new** instruction, writing topics, and writing prompts for reading-based writing as the summary, reaction, and two-part response for assignments to help students write with more substance and become better prepared to write across the curriculum and to avoid plagiarism
- A **new** discussion on the kinds of paragraphs taught in this book: introductory, developmental (with its stand-alone circumstantial nature), transitional, and concluding
- **Enhanced** mode-specific boxes of transitional words in ten chapters
- **Updated** lists of reading-based, general, cross-curricular, and career-related topics and prompts in Chapters 6–15
- **Refined** MLA and APA guides for documented writing research are available on the *At a Glance* Student Companion Site and Instructor Companion Site
- An abundance of **refined** printable quizzes on the Instructor Companion Site (for sentence writing keyed to the Handbook—diagnostic, final, and unit quizzes)

∿ The At a Glance Series

At a Glance: Writing Paragraphs and Beyond with Integrated Readings is the second-level book in the bestselling At a Glance series. Along with *At a Glance: Writing Essays and Beyond with Integrated Readings* and *At a Glance: Reader*, it meets the current need for concise, comprehensive, and contemporary textbooks that students can afford. All four books provide basic instruction, exercises, and writing assignments at the designated level, as well as support material for instructors. *At a Glance: Sentences* and *At a Glance: Paragraphs* include a transition to the next level of writing, and each of *At a Glance: Paragraphs, At a Glance: Essays, and At a Glance: Reader* ends with a handbook that students can refer to for help with sentence-level issues or for problems with mechanics and spelling. *At a Glance: Reader* presents brief writing instruction and thirty sources for reading-based writing. Each book in the At a Glance series can be used alone, with one of the other At a Glance books, or with another textbook. Two or more At a Glance books can be shrink-wrapped and delivered at a discount. As a special offer, *At a Glance: Reader* is half price when shrink-wrapped with another At a Glance book.

∿ Instructional Approach

Using explanation, student examples, exercises, and applications, *At a Glance: Essays* presents the writing process in Chapters 1–2, in a study in the similarity between developmental paragraphs (especially stand-alone paragraphs) and essays in Chapter 3, techniques of critical reading in Chapter 4, and forms of reading-based writing in Chapter 5. Each of Chapters 6 through 15 uses the same sequence of instruction: a writing strategy for a particular pattern, a box of transitional terms, an exercise that gives students practice in organizing the pattern, student examples and professional examples with questions for students to answer and discuss, topic suggestions (reading-based, cross-curricular, career-related, and general topics) for writing such paragraphs or short essays, and a concluding summary of guidelines specific to the pattern. The Handbook presents sentence writing instruction: capitalization, grammar, punctuation, spelling, and other fundamentals.

∿ Support Material for Instructors

- **Instructor's Guide for *At a Glance*.** The Instructor's Guide available online within the Instructor Companion Site provides helpful hints for teaching *At a Glance* in the classroom. It includes sample syllabi, suggestions for working with basic writing students and ESL students, grading tips, Answer Keys, quizzes on sentence writing, readings, and more.

- **Instructor Companion Site for *At a Glance*.** The instructor site provides helpful resources in addition to the Instructor's Guide, such as PowerPoint slides, at *login.cengage.com*.
- **Student Companion Site for *At a Glance* at *www.cengagebrain.com*.** The student site provides helpful resources, an MLA guide and an APA guide to documented papers, printable enlarged worksheets and guides, tips on writing resumes and letters of application, suggestions for taking tests, and more.

Acknowledgments

We are profoundly indebted to the many instructors who have reviewed *At a Glance: Paragraphs* for these six editions and helped it grow and remain fresh, vibrant, and innovative. Here are a few of those thoughtful and imaginative reviewers: Darin Cozzens, Surry Community College; Paul Peterson, William Rainey Harper College: Harvey Rubenstein, Hudson County Community College: Connie A. Gramza, Erie Community College; Janice Hart, Central New Mexico Community College; Charlotte Laughlin, McLennan Community College; Buzz R. Pounds, Lewis University; Cindi Clarke, Belmont Technical College; Tim Kelley, Northwest-Shoals Community College; James Crooks, Shasta College; Joanne Kara, Pennsylvania Institute of Technology; Howard Sage, Hunter College; Denton Tulloch, Miami Dade College; Karen J. Weyant, Jamestown Community College; Deborah Burson-Smith, Southern University at New Orleans; David Lang, Golden Gate University; Kathy Masters, Arkansas State University; Steve Stremmel, American River College; and Anne-Marie Williams, Cuesta College.

We also deeply appreciate the expert, dedicated work of freelance production manager Nancy Benjamin with Books By Design, editorial specialist Ann Marie Radaskiewicz McNeely, permissions editor Christina Taylor, principal editor Margaret Manos, and our colleagues at Cengage Learning: Annie Todd, Elizabeth Rice, Luria Rittenberg, Ann Hoffman, and Aimee Bear.

Lee Brandon
Kelly Brandon

～ Student Overview

This book is designed to help you write better paragraphs and short essays. Chapters 1 and 2 focus on the writing process itself. You'll discover prewriting techniques to help you get started, and you'll learn ways to develop, revise, and edit your drafts until you produce polished compositions. Chapter 3 discusses the essay in relation to the paragraph and can help you expand some of your paragraphs into essays. Chapter 4 explains how to read critically, and Chapter 5 teaches skills in writing summaries and critiques of reading selections.

Each of Chapters 6 through 15 describes a different pattern for developing an effective paragraph. In your other classes, at work, and in your private life, you will have occasions to write in particular ways. Usually you will be expected to blend the forms of that writing. This book offers you directions, suggestions on using those forms, and examples. Chapter 6, for instance, is about narration; Chapter 7 is about description; Chapter 8 is about exemplification—that is, the use of examples. Chapter 11 discusses cause and effect, and Chapter 15 presents the art of argument. All of those chapters include sample paragraphs written by students and professional writers. Altogether you will study ten patterns of thought and their necessary combinations. At the end, the Handbook is available for help when you need assistance in capitalization, grammar, punctuation, spelling, and much more.

Here are some strategies to help you make the best use of this book and to accelerate your mastery of writing skills so that you can always get full credit for the communication of what you have to say.

1. **Evaluate your writing skills.** On the inside front cover of this book, you will find the **Self-Evaluation Chart for the Brandon Guide** for you to use in recording problems and progress in revising and editing. On page A-1, the facing page, you will see a list of the elements of the **Brandon Guide for Revising and Editing** in the form of two acronyms. **CLUESS** (pronounced "clues" for easy memorization) represents Coherence, Language, Unity, Emphasis, Support, and Sentences for revision. **CGPS**

(pronounced "see GPS") represents **C**apitalization, **G**rammar, **P**unctuation, and **S**pelling for editing. Each element is keyed with page numbers to instruction in this book. Those ten elements in the acronyms are essential for effective revising and editing. They can guide you in all writing situations and in reflections on the results of that writing. The two acronyms can also provide a framework and foundation for peer editing, cooperative projects, and student-instructor conferences.

Drawing especially on your instructor's comments on your work, you can pencil in matters that need your attention and their location in this book. For page numbers of solutions to common writing problems, use the Brandon Guide for Revising and Editing on A-1, the facing page; the Index at the end of the book; and the Correction Chart just inside the back cover. As you master a persistent problem, you can place a checkmark, or perhaps a star, alongside it as a badge of dedication to learning.

Here is a partially completed Self-Evaluation Chart with some brief guidelines for filling out your chart.

Self-Evaluation Chart for the Brandon Guide

Drawing on your instructor's comments, list persistent problems with page number references to matching instruction in this book. Add to your lists throughout the term to note needs and then to show progress as you become more proficient and confident.

Revise with CLUESS (pronounced as "clues")

Coherence	Language	Unity	Emphasis	Support	Sentences
Use transitions, p. 185	No trite words, p. 23	Topic sentence, p. 12	Repeat key word, p. 23	Use examples, p. 88	Vary sentence beginnings, p. 188

Edit with CGPS (pronounced as "see GPS")

Capitalization: I'm studying biology, English, and math. p. 211

Grammar: Pronoun case: between you and me. . . . p. 200

Punctuation: After she left, I cried. p. 206

Spelling: It's or its? There or their? Receive or receive? p. 216

2. **Use the Brandon Writing Process Worksheet** that appears on page A-2. As directed by your instructor, enlarge and copy the worksheet, and record details about each of your assignments, such as the due date, topic, length, and form. The worksheet will also remind you of the stages of the writing process: Explore, Organize, and Write. An enlarged, printable copy is online on your Student Companion Site at *www.cengagebrain.com.*

3. **Be positive.** All the elements you record in your Self-Evaluation Chart are covered in *At a Glance: Writing Paragraphs and Beyond.* The index, and the Correction Chart on the inside back cover of the book will direct you to the additional instruction you decide you need. An enlarged, printable copy of the chart is available online at the Student Companion Site at *www .cengagebrain.com.* Soon, seeing what you have mastered and checked off your list will give you a much-deserved sense of accomplishment.

Finally, don't compare yourself with others. Compare yourself with yourself and, as you make progress, consider yourself what you are—a student on the path toward more effective writing, a student on the path toward college success.

1

The Paragraph
and Prewriting

∿ The Paragraph Defined

Definition: A paragraph includes one or more sentences that state or develop an idea. The length, shape, and organization of an effective paragraph are determined by its standards and purpose. A paragraph within the typical college essay fulfills one of these four purposes:

Introductory: Usually the first paragraph in an essay, the introductory paragraph gives the necessary background and indicates the main idea, called the **thesis**.

Developmental: A unit of several sentences, the developmental paragraph expands on an idea. This book features the writing of the developmental paragraph. When written by itself, as it frequently is for college writing assignments and tests, the developmental paragraph often resembles a miniature essay in structure.

Transitional: Usually a brief paragraph of one or two sentences, the transitional paragraph merely directs the reader from one point in an essay to another.

Concluding: Usually the last paragraph in an essay, the concluding paragraph makes the final comment on the topic.

∿ The Stand-Alone Paragraph

If a developmental paragraph is submitted for an assignment or published alone, it is called a **stand-alone paragraph**. For college classes, a teacher in any discipline may direct you write a short discussion, or paragraph, on an "essay" test. Specifically, in an English class, an instructor may assign paragraphs to teach overall organization, development, and correctness of effective writing. If so, those will be stand-alone developmental paragraphs. In textbooks such as this one, you will also read stand-alone paragraphs by student and professional writers, paragraphs that serve as models for good writing and as subject material for your reflection, for in-class discussions, and for reading-based writing.

If those paragraphs were written by professional authors, they were legally extracted (with credit given) from essays, articles, or books and published as stand-alone paragraphs in textbooks. In this book the first model student paragraph, used with permission, was written as a single assignment. As a stand-alone paragraph, it focuses on why Magic Johnson was an excellent professional basketball player. Given more time—and perhaps with research— that same topic might have become an introduction or a conclusion for a longer work, such as an essay or book, or might have become an essay or book itself.

◯ The Stand-Alone Developmental Paragraph

Writing stand-alone paragraphs will give you practice in working with structure, support, focus, and correctness. Doing so can also prepare you for writing longer compositions, such as essays and research papers. The suggested topics and the range of words for a single assignment will guide you in the extent and focus of the development of your subject. In a writing class, you might be asked to compose a paragraph that does not exceed, say, a single written page or is limited to a stated number of words.

Paragraph Design

Typically, paragraphs written as college assignments are easy to identify because they are indented. Each one starts with skipped spaces at the beginning of the first line. The developmental paragraph featured in this book contains three parts: the subject, the topic sentence, and the support.

The **subject** is what you will write about. At the outset, the subject is likely to be broad or general, and, therefore, must be focused.

The **topic sentence** provides the focus for that subject by specifying what you intend to *do* with the subject.

Paragraph Patterns

The topic sentence contains the central, or main, idea of the paragraph. Everything else in the paragraph supports the topic sentence; that is, all the other sentences explain or say more about the central idea. The **support** is the evidence or reasoning that fulfills, or justifies, the topic sentence. That support can be developed according to several basic patterns of thought. Each of ten patterns is the subject of one chapter of this book. The following questions can help you choose an appropriate pattern or a combination of patterns for your paragraph of development.

> *Narration:* Can you illustrate your point by telling a story?
>
> *Description:* How does something look, sound, feel, taste, or smell?
>
> *Exemplification:* Can you support your main idea with examples of what you mean?
>
> *Analysis by division:* What are the parts of a unit, and how do they work together?
>
> *Process analysis:* How do you do something? How is (was) something done?
>
> *Cause and effect:* What are the reasons for or the results of an event, a trend, or a circumstance?
>
> *Classification:* How do you group items or ideas according to similarities?
>
> *Comparison and contrast:* How are two or more subjects similar and different?
>
> *Definition:* What does a term mean?
>
> *Argument:* What evidence and reasoning will convince someone that you are right?

These patterns are usually combined in writing paragraphs and essays, though one pattern will often provide the overarching structure. Regardless of the pattern or combination you use, the definition of the developmental paragraph remains the same. A **developmental paragraph**, **stand-alone** or otherwise, is a group of sentences, each with the function of supporting a single main idea, which is contained in the topic sentence.

A Sample Professional Paragraph

Here is a brief example of a paragraph by a professional writer:

A cat's tail is a good barometer of its intentions. An excited or aggressively aroused cat will whip its entire tail back and forth. When I talk to Sam, he holds up his end of the conversation by occasionally flicking the tip of his tail. Mother cats move their tails back and forth to invite their kittens to play. A kitten raises its tail perpendicularly to beg for attention; older cats may do so to beg for food. When your cat holds its tail aloft while crisscrossing in front of you, it is trying to say, "Follow me"—usually to the kitchen, or more precisely, to the refrigerator. Unfortunately, many cats have endangered their tails in refrigerator doors as a consequence.

—*Michael W. Fox*, "What Is Your Pet Trying to Tell You?"

The paragraph begins with the topic sentence: "A cat's tail is a good barometer of its intentions." The other sentences provide support for the topic sentence; they give examples to show that the topic sentence is credible. The final sentence adds whimsy to the writing and provides a sense of ending, or closure, to the discussion. One often-effective technique is to use a phrase in the conclusion that repeats or echoes one at the beginning of the paragraph.

Although the topic sentence is often the first sentence of the paragraph, it does not have to be. Furthermore, the topic sentence is sometimes restated or echoed at the end of the paragraph, although again it does not have to be. However, a well-phrased concluding sentence can emphasize the central idea of the paragraph as well as provide a nice balance and ending.

A paragraph is not a constraining formula; in fact, it has variations. In some instances, for example, the topic sentence is not found in a single sentence. It may be the combination of two sentences, or it may be an easily understood but unwritten underlying idea that unifies the paragraph. Nevertheless, the paragraph in most college writing contains discussion supporting a stated topic sentence, and the instruction in this book is based on that fundamental idea.

A Sample Student Paragraph

The following paragraph was written by college student Cyrus Norton. The topic sentence, including the subject of the paragraph and the focus of the paragraph, has been underlined. Norton's topic sentence (not the first sentence, in this instance), his support of the topic sentence, and his concluding sentence have been identified in the margin. This is the final draft. Following it, we will back up and, in this chapter and the next, show how Norton moved during the writing process from his initial idea to this final paragraph.

Magic Johnson, an NBA Great

Cyrus Norton

Some NBA (National Basketball Association) players are good because they have a special talent in one area. <u>Magic</u>

Topic sentence <u>Johnson was a great NBA star because he was</u> <u>excellent in shooting, passing, rebounding,</u>

Support for shooting <u>and leading.</u> As a shooter, few have ever equaled him. He could slam, shovel, hook, and fire from three-point range—all with deadly accuracy. As for free throws, he led all NBA players in shooting percentage in 1988-89. While averaging more than twenty

Support for passing points per game, he helped others become stars with his passes. As the point guard (the quarterback of basketball), he was always near the top in the league in assists and was famous for his "no-look" pass, which often surprised even his teammates with its precision. When he wasn't shooting or

Support for rebounding passing, he was rebounding. A top rebounding guard is unusual in professional basketball, but Magic, at six feet, nine inches, could bump shoulders and leap with anyone. These three qualities made him probably the most spectacular triple-double threat of all time. "Triple-double" means reaching two digits in scoring, assists, and rebounding.

Support for leading

Magic didn't need more for greatness in the NBA, but he had more. With his everlasting smile and boundless energy, he was also an inspirational team leader. He always believed in himself and his team. When his team was down by a point and three seconds remained on the game clock, the fans looked for Magic to get the ball. They watched as he dribbled once, he faded, he leaped, he twisted, and he hooked one in from twenty feet! That was

Concluding sentence

magic. That was Magic.

Let's consider Norton's paragraph in the light of what we know about paragraphs in general. Magic Johnson, the subject, is what the paragraph is all about. In this example, the title also names the subject. The topic sentence, the unifying and controlling idea, makes a clear statement about what the writer will say about the subject. As usual, the topic sentence appears near the beginning of the paragraph. The support gives evidence and examples to back up the controlling idea. The last sentence, "That was Magic," echoes the topic sentence by highlighting his greatness. It is usually called the concluding sentence, or statement.

The author has told you what he was going to say, he has said it, and finally he has reminded you of what he has told you. The concluding sentence is sometimes omitted. The two most common designs of developmental paragraphs in college writing are these:

Topic sentence → support → concluding sentence
Topic sentence → support

"Magic Johnson, an NBA Great" is a typical paragraph: a group of sentences that present and develop an idea. As for most compositions Norton prepared for his academic classes, Norton wrote in **third-person point of view,** meaning he focused on his subject, Magic Johnson, and wrote about him from a detached perspective. Norton did not refer to himself with first-person pronouns such as *I, me, my,* or *mine,* or address his readers with second-person pronouns such as *you* or *your.* Instead, he referred to Magic Johnson by name or used *he, him,* and other third-person pronouns.

Principles at a Glance

Developmental paragraph:	A group of sentences that present and develop an idea.
Topic sentence:	The sentence that expresses the controlling idea of the paragraph. The topic sentence mentions the subject (what the paragraph is about) and the focus (what the writer will say about the subject).
Support:	Evidence, such as details, examples, analysis, and other discussion, that explains the topic sentence.
Basic paragraph designs:	Topic sentence → support → concluding sentence Topic sentence → support

⌒ The Writing Process

Writing does not mean merely putting words on paper. It is a process that often involves several steps: using prewriting techniques to explore a topic, limiting and then developing the topic, making an outline, writing a draft, revising the draft as many times as necessary, and editing. Writers sometimes discover that their topic sentence or their outline does not work, and they go back and alter their original concept or design.

For flexible, systematic guidance, consider using the Brandon Writing Process Worksheet on page A-2. It can be copied, enlarged, and submitted with your assignment if your instructor asks you to do so. It also can be printed in an enlarged form from the Student Companion Site at www.cengagebrain.com.

⌒ Prewriting: Using the Blank Sheet of Opportunity

Certain strategies commonly grouped under the heading *prewriting* can help you get started and develop your ideas. Actually, these strategies—freewriting, brainstorming, clustering, defining a topic, and outlining—are very much a part of writing. The understandable desire to skip to the finished statement is what causes the most common student-writer grief: that of not filling the blank sheet or of filling it but not significantly improving on the void. The prewriting strategies that follow will help you attack the blank sheet constructively with imaginative thought, analysis, and experimentation. They can lead to clear, effective communication.

Although the strategies can work very well, you do not need to use all of them in all writing assignments. Learn them now, and use them when they are needed. Think of this approach as carrying a box of tools and then selecting the best tools for the job.

Freewriting

Freewriting is an exercise that its originator, Peter Elbow, has called "babbling in print." In freewriting, you write without stopping, letting your ideas tumble forth. You do not concern yourself with the fundamentals of writing, such as punctuation and spelling. Freewriting is an adventure into your memory and imagination. It is concerned with discovery, invention, and exploration. If you are at a loss for words on your subject, write in a comment such as "I don't know what is coming next" or "blah, blah, blah," and continue when relevant words come. It is important to keep writing. Freewriting immediately eliminates the blank page and thereby helps you break through an emotional barrier, but that is not the only benefit. The words that you sort through in your freewriting will include some you can use. You can then underline or circle those words and even add notes on the side so that the freewriting continues to grow even after its initial spontaneous expression.

The way you proceed depends on the type of assignment: working with a topic of your choice, working from a restricted list of topics, or working with a prescribed topic.

Working with the *topic of your choice* affords you the greatest freedom of exploration. You would probably select a subject that interests you and freewrite about it, allowing your mind to wander among its many parts, perhaps mixing fact and fantasy, direct experience, and hearsay. A freewriting about music might uncover areas of special interest and knowledge, such as jazz, rap, metal, rock, or folk rock, that you would want to pursue further in freewriting or other prewriting strategies.

Working from a *restricted list* requires a more focused freewriting. With the list, you can, of course, experiment with several topics to discover what is most suitable for you. If, for example, "career choice," "career preparation," "career guidance," and "career prospects" are on the restricted list, you would probably select one and freewrite about it. If it works well for you, you would probably proceed with the next step of your prewriting. If you are not satisfied with what you uncover in freewriting, you would explore another item from the restricted list.

When working with a *prescribed topic*, you focus on a particular topic and try to restrict your freewriting to its boundaries. If your topic specifies a division of a subject area such as "political involvement of your generation," then you would tie those key words to your own information, critical thinking, and imaginative responses. If the topic is restricted to, say, your reaction to a particular reading selection such as a poem, then that poem would give you the framework for your free associations with your own experiences, creations, and opinions.

Most of your college writing will be in the **third-person point of view,** meaning you will analyze your subject (an article, a section of a book, a set of readings, or an idea you research) and write about it from a detached point of view, not referring to yourself by using first-person words such as *I, me,* or *my* or by using second-person words such as *you* or *your.*

You should learn to use freewriting because it will often serve you well, but you need not use it every time you write. Some very short writing assignments do not call for freewriting. An in-class assignment may not allow time for freewriting.

Nevertheless, freewriting is often a useful strategy in your toolbox of writing techniques. It can help you get words on paper, break emotional barriers, generate topics, develop new insights, and explore ideas.

Freewriting can lead to other stages of prewriting and writing, and it can also provide content as you develop your topic.

The following example of freewriting, and the writing, revising, and editing examples in Chapter 2, are from student Cyrus Norton's paragraph, "Magic Johnson, an NBA Great" (p. 5). Norton's topic came from a restricted list; he was directed to write about the success of an individual. Had he been working with a prescribed topic, he might have been directed to concentrate on a specific aspect of Johnson's career, such as business, philanthropy, public service, baseball team management (Los Angeles Dodgers), or the one Norton chose: great basketball playing.

Sample Freewriting

great   Magic Johnson was the <u>greatest</u> player
                I've ever seen in professional basketball.
leader   Actually not just a player but a <u>leader</u> and an
inspiration   <u>inspiration</u> to the team so they always gave
                him the ball when the game was on the line.

	It was too bad his career was cut short when
	they discovered he was HIV positive. Actually
	he came back but then retired again. He made
rich	<u>a lot of money</u> and I guess he invested it
	wisely because his name is linked to the Lakers
	and theaters and more. Also to programs making
	people aware of the danger of AIDS and helping
	kids grow up and stay out of trouble. But the
playing	main thing about Magic is the <u>way he played</u>. He
	could do everything. He even played center one
scoring	time in a championship game. He always <u>scored</u>
passing	<u>a lot</u> and he could <u>pass</u> like nobody else. Even
	though he was a guard, he was tall and could
rebounding	<u>rebound</u>. He was great. Everyone says so.

After doing this freewriting, Cyrus Norton went back through his work looking for ideas to develop for a writing assignment. As he recognized those ideas, he underlined key words and phrases and made a few notes in the margins. By reading only the underlined words, you can obtain a basic understanding of what is important to him. It is not necessary to underline entire sentences.

In addition to putting some words on that dreaded blank sheet of paper, Norton discovered that he had quite a lot of information about Magic Johnson and that he had selected a favorable topic to develop. The entire process took little time. Had he found few or no promising ideas, he might have freewritten about another topic. In going back through his work, he saw some errors in writing, but he did not correct them because the main purpose of freewriting is discovery, not correct grammar, punctuation, or spelling. He was confident that he could then continue with the process of writing a paper.

Brainstorming

Brainstorming features key words and phrases that relate in various ways to the subject area or to the specific topic you are concerned with. One effective way to get started is to ask the big six questions about your subject area: *Who? What? Where? When? Why?* and *How?* Then let your mind run free as you jot down answers in single entries or lists. Some of the big six questions may not fit, and some may be more important than others, depending on the purposes of your writing. For example, if you were writing about the causes of a situation, the *Why?* question could be more important than the others; if you were concerned with how to do something, the *How?* question would predominate. If you were writing in response to a reading selection, you would confine your thinking to questions appropriately related to the content of that reading selection, probably writing responses in third person as you focus on the subject outside yourself.

Whatever your focus for the questions is, the result is likely to be numerous ideas that will provide information for continued exploration and development of your topic. Thus your pool of information for writing widens and deepens.

An alternative to asking the big six questions is simply to make a list of words and phrases related to your subject area or specific topic. That technique, favored by many professional writers and scholars, is called **listing**.

Cyrus Norton continued with the topic of Magic Johnson and he tightened his topic to focus on particular areas. Although Norton could have listed the annotations and the words he underlined in his freewriting, he used the big six questions for his framework.

Who?	Magic Johnson
What?	great basketball player
Where?	the NBA
When?	for more than ten years
Why?	love of game and great talent
How?	shooting, passing, rebounding, leading, coolness, inspiring

As it turned out, *How?* was the most fruitful question for Norton, and it led him to a list.

Clustering

Clustering (also called **mapping**) is yet another prewriting technique. Start by double-bubbling your topic; that is, write it down in the middle of the page and draw a double circle around it. Then respond to the question "What comes to mind?" Single-bubble other ideas on spokes radiating from the hub that contains the topic. Any bubble can lead to another bubble or numerous bubbles in the same way. This strategy is sometimes used instead of or before making an outline to organize and develop ideas.

The more focused the topic inside the double bubble, the fewer the number of spokes that will radiate with single bubbles. For example, a topic such as "high school dropouts" would have more spokes than "reasons for dropping out of high school."

Here is Cyrus Norton's cluster on the subject of Magic Johnson.

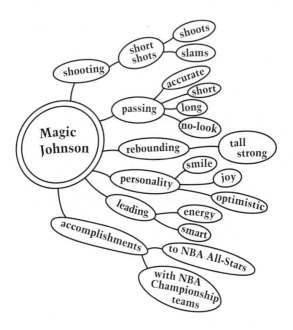

~ Writing the Topic Sentence

The topic sentence is the most important sentence in your prewriting and also in your paragraph. It includes two parts: the subject and the focus (what you will do with your subject). Consider, for example, this topic sentence:

<u>Magic Johnson</u> <u>was a great all-around NBA player.</u>
    subject   focus

It is an effective topic sentence because it limits the subject and indicates focus that can be developed in additional sentences. Another sound version is the following, which goes further to include divisions for the focus.

<u>Magic Johnson</u> <u>was a great NBA star because he was excellent</u>
    subject   focus

in shooting, passing, rebounding, and leading.

Ineffective topic sentences are often too broad, vague, or too narrow.

VAGUE   Magic Johnson was everything to everybody.

TOO BROAD Magic Johnson was fun.

           Magic Johnson was a success in basketball.

TOO NARROW Magic Johnson went to Michigan State
           University.

           Magic Johnson signed a professional basketball
           contract with the Los Angeles Lakers.

Usually, simple statements of fact do not need or do not allow for development.

Exercise 1 Evaluating Topic Sentences

Mark the following statements for subject (S) and focus (F), and label each as effective (E) or ineffective (I). Effective statements are those that you can easily relate to supporting evidence. Ineffective statements are vague, too broad, or too narrow.

_____ 1. Columbus is located in Ohio.

_____ 2. Columbus is a fabulous city.

_____ 3. Columbus has dealt thoroughly with its housing problems.

_____ 4. A monkey is a primate.

_____ 5. Monkeys are fun.

_____ 6. In clinical studies, monkeys have demonstrated a remarkable ability to reason.

_____ 7. More than a million cats are born in California each year.

_____ 8. A simple observation of a domesticated cat in the pursuit of game will show that it has not lost its instinct for survival.

_____ 9. The two teams in the Rose Bowl have similar records.

_____ 10. Michigan State is in the Rose Bowl.

Exercise 2   Writing Topic Sentences

Complete the following entries by making each into a solid topic sentence. Only a subject and part of the focus are provided. The missing part may be more than a single word.

EXAMPLE: Car salespersons behave differently depending on <u>the car they are selling and the kind of customer they are serving.</u>

1. Television commercials are often _____.

2. Rap music promotes _____.

3. My part-time job taught me _____.

4. I promote environmental conservation by _____.

5. The clothing that a person wears often suggests _____.

6. My close friend is preoccupied with _____.

7. Winning a lot of money is not always _____.

8. Country music appeals to our most basic _____.

9. Friendship depends on _____.

10. A good salesperson should _____.

Exercise 3   Writing Topic Sentences

Write a topic sentence for each of the following subjects.

1. Computer literacy _____.

2. My taste in music _____.

3. Bus transportation _____.

4. The fear of crime _____.

5. An excellent boss _____.

6. Doing well in college English classes _____.

7. Violence on television _____.

8. Child-care centers _____.

9. Good health _____.

10. Teenage voters _____.

〜 Writing the Outline

An **outline** is a pattern for showing the relationship of ideas. The two main outline forms are the **sentence outline** (each entry is a complete sentence) and the **topic outline** (each entry is a key word or phrase). The topic outline is commonly used for both paragraphs and essays.

Indentation, number and letter sequences, punctuation, and the placement of words are important to clear communication in an outline. We do not read an outline expecting to be surprised by form and content, as we do a poem. We go to the outline for information, and we expect to find ideas easily. Unconventional marks (circles, squares, half-parentheses) and items out of order are distracting and, therefore, undesirable in an outline. The standard form is as easily mastered as a nonstandard form, and it is worth your time to learn it. Outlining is not difficult: The pattern is flexible and can have any number of levels and parts.

Basically, an outline shows how a topic sentence is supported. Thus it shows the organization of the paragraph. The most important supporting material, called the **major support**, is indicated by Roman numerals. That major support is developed by less important supporting material, called the **minor support**, which in turn may be developed by details or examples. Here is the outline developed by Cyrus Norton:

Magic Johnson was a great NBA star because he was excellent in shooting, passing, rebounding, and leading.

I. Shooting (major support)
   A. Short shots (minor support)
      1. Shovel (detail)
      2. Slam-dunk (detail)
   B. Long shots (minor support)
   C. Free throws (minor support)

II. Passing (major support)
   A. No-look (minor support)
   B. Precise (minor support)

III. Rebounding (major support)
   A. Leaping (minor support)
   B. Bumping shoulders (minor support)

IV. Leading (major support)
   A. Energy (minor support)

B. Spirit (minor support)
  1. Faith (detail)
  2. Smile (detail)

The foundation of a good outline and hence a good paragraph is a
strong topic sentence, which means one with a specific subject and
a well-defined focus. After writing a good topic sentence, the next
step is to divide the focus into parts. Just what the parts are will depend on what you specify in the focus. Consider the thought process
involved. What sections of material would be appropriate in your
discussion to support or explain that topic sentence?

Among the most common forms of division are the following:

- Divisions of time or incident to tell a story

  I. Situation
  II. Conflict
  III. Struggle
  IV. Outcome
  V. Meaning

- Divisions of examples or divisions of one example into three or
  more aspects

  I. First example (aspect)
  II. Second example (aspect)
  III. Third example (aspect)

- Divisions of causes or effects

  I. Cause (or effect) one
  II. Cause (or effect) two
  III. Cause (or effect) three

- Divisions of a unit into parts (such as the federal government into
  executive, legislative, and judicial branches—or Magic Johnson's
  all-around skill into shooting, passing, rebounding, and leading)

  I. Part one
  II. Part two
  III. Part three

- Divisions of how to do something or how something was done

  I. Preparation
  II. Steps
    A. Step 1
    B. Step 2
    C. Step 3

Exercise 4 Completing Basic Outline Patterns

Fill in the missing outline parts. Consider whether you are dealing with time, examples, causes, effects, parts, or steps. Answers will vary, depending on individual experiences and views.

1. Too many of us are preoccupied with material things.

   I. Clothing

   II. Cars

   III. _____

2. Television sitcoms may vary, but every successful show has certain components.

   I. Good acting

   II. _____

   III. Good situations

   IV. _____

3. A female who is trying to discourage unwanted sexual advances should take several measures.

   I. _____

   II. Set clear boundaries

   III. Avoid compromising situations

4. Concentrating during reading involves various techniques.

   I. Preview material

   II. Pose questions

   III. _____

5. Crime has some bad effects on a neighborhood.

   I. People fearful

      A. Don't go out at night

      B. _____

   II. People without love for neighborhood

      A. _____

      B. Put houses up for sale

   III. People as victims

      A. Loss of possessions

      B. _____

6. Exercising can improve a person's life.

    I. Looks better

      A. Skin

      B. _____

   II. Feels better

      A. _____

      B. Body

   III. Performs better

      A. Work

      B. _____

7. Shoppers in department stores can be grouped according to needs.

    I. _____

   II. Special-needs shoppers

   III. Bargain hunters

8. There are different kinds of intelligence based on situations.

    I. Street-smart

   II. Common sense

   III. _____

9. Smoking should be discouraged.

    I. Harm to smokers

      A. _____

      B. Cancer risk

   II. Harm to those around smokers

      A. _____

      B. Fellow workers

III. Cost

    A. Industry—production and absenteeism

    B. _____

Writer's Guidelines at a Glance: The Paragraph and Prewriting

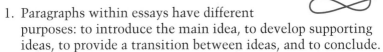

1. Paragraphs within essays have different purposes: to introduce the main idea, to develop supporting ideas, to provide a transition between ideas, and to conclude.
2. A paragraph submitted or published by itself is called a **stand-alone paragraph**.
3. By far the most common form of paragraphs in college writing is the **developmental**, which is the main structural concern of this book. A common form for the stand-alone paragraph, it is a group of sentences, each with the function of stating or supporting a single controlling idea contained in the topic sentence.
4. The **topic sentence** expresses the controlling idea of the paragraph. It has a subject (what the paragraph is about) and a focus (what the writer intends to do with the subject).
5. The support is the evidence, such as details, examples, and explanations, that backs up the topic sentence.
6. Writing developmental paragraphs will give you practice in working with structure, support, focus, and correctness, and can also prepare you for writing longer compositions such as essays and research papers.
7. Most college writing will be in the **third-person point of view,** meaning you will analyze your subject and write about it from a detached perspective, usually not referring to yourself with first-person pronouns such as *I, me, we, us, my, mine, our,* or *ours,* or by using second-person pronouns such as *you* or *your,* unless you are telling your audience how to do something.
8. The two most common developmental paragraph designs in college writing are these:

   ▪ Topic sentence → support → concluding sentence
   ▪ Topic sentence → support

9. Prewriting includes activities you do before writing your first draft or whenever you need new ideas.

- **Freewriting:** writing without stopping, letting your ideas tumble forth. Freewriting helps you break emotional barriers, generate topics, and discover and explore ideas.
- **Brainstorming:** a listing procedure that helps you discover key words and phrases that relate to your topic. Simply make a list, or ask *Who? What? Where? When? Why?* and How? questions of your topic.
- **Clustering:** a graphic way of showing connections and relationships. Start by double-bubbling your topic. Then ask "What comes to mind?" and single-bubble other ideas on spokes radiating from the double bubble.

10. The **outline** is a form for indicating the relationship of ideas. An outline shows how a topic sentence is supported. Thus it reveals the organization of the paragraph. Major support is indicated by Roman numerals. The major support is developed by minor support, which in turn may be developed by details or examples.

Topic sentence

  I. Major support

    A. Minor support
    B. Minor support
      1. Details or examples
      2. Details or examples

  II. Major support

    A. Minor support
    B. Minor support

11. Systematic revision and editing are essential to good writing.
12. Consider using the Brandon Writing Process Worksheet as a guide to your writing.

2

Writing, Revising, and Editing the Paragraph

Writing Your First Draft

Once you have completed your topic sentence and outline (or list or cluster), you are ready to begin writing your paragraph. The initial writing is called the **first**, or **rough**, **draft**. Your topic sentence is likely to be at or near the beginning of your paragraph and will be followed by your support as ordered by your outline.

Paying close attention to your outline for basic organization, you should proceed without worrying about the refinements of writing. This is not the time to concern yourself with perfect spelling, grammar, or punctuation. After you have finished that first draft, take a close look at it. If your topic sentence is sound and your outline has served you well, you have a basic discussion. You have made a statement and supported it, and you are on your way to writing an effective paragraph.

The Recursive Factor

The entire process of writing can be called **recursive**, which means "going back and forth." In this respect, writing is like reading. If you do not understand what you have read, you back up and read it again. After you have reread a passage, you may still need to read selectively. The same can be said of writing. If, for example, after having developed an outline and started writing your first draft, you discover that your subject is too broad, you should back up, narrow your topic sentence, and then adjust your outline. The term *first draft* suggests quite accurately that there will be other drafts, or versions, of your writing. Only in a dire situation, such as an in-class examination when you have time for only one draft, should you be satisfied with a single effort. You may even decide to return to an early list or cluster of ideas to see how you can use a smaller grouping of those ideas. Revision is usually the most recursive of all parts of the writing process. You will go over your material again and again until you are satisfied that you have expressed yourself as well as you possibly can. This book provides an easily mastered system for revising and editing: The Brandon Guide for Revising and Editing.

～ The Brandon Guide for Revising and Editing

What you do beyond the first draft is revising and editing. The Brandon Guide for Revising and Editing is a system that includes writing from idea to final statement. It has two parts. **Revising** involves reviewing the material for organization, content, and language effectiveness. **Editing** involves making final corrections of mistakes in matters such as capitalization, grammar, punctuation, and spelling. In practice, editing and revising are not always separate activities, although writers usually wait until the next-to-the-last draft to identify and repair many of the problems with the fundamentals of writing, the ones that can be easily overlooked if one does not scrutinize the material.

The Brandon Guide for Revising and Editing applies to all parts of this book. The first two pages inside the front cover provide charts for recording your needs and accomplishments as you write paragraphs and short essays.

Revising with CLUESS

To help you recall key features of skillful writing as you enrich and repair your first draft, the Brandon Guide offers an acronym in which each letter suggests an important element of good writing for effective revision. The acronym is **CLUESS** (pronounce as "clues" for easy memorization), which provides reminders, or a checklist, for **c**oherence, **l**anguage, **u**nity, **e**mphasis, **s**upport, and **s**entences. This mnemonic device enables you to memorize the features of good writing quickly. These features need not be attended to only one at a time or addressed in a particular order as you revise your writing.

Coherence: Connect your ideas. (See p. A-1 for page numbers.)

- Are the ideas clearly related, one to each and each to all?
- Is there a clear pattern of organization (time, space, or emphasis)?
- Is the pattern supported by transitional words (shown in a boxed list in each of Chapters 6–15) that suggest the basis of that organization (time: *now, then, later;* space: *above, below, up, down;* emphasis: *first, second, last*)?
- Is coherence enhanced by the use of transitional terms, pronouns, repetition, and a consistent point of view?

Language: Use words appropriate for your purpose and audience. (See p. A-1 for page numbers.)

- Is the general style of language use appropriate (properly standard and formal or informal) for the purpose of the piece and the intended audience?
- Is the tone (language use showing attitude toward material and audience) appropriate?
- Is the point of view clear and consistent (first, second, or—for most academic writing—third person)?
- Is the word choice (diction) effective? Are the words precise in conveying meaning? Are they fresh and not overused and trite?

Unity: Stay on your topic. (See p. A-1 for page numbers.)

- Are the thesis and every topic sentence clear and well stated? Do they indicate both subject and focus?
- Are all points of support clearly related to and subordinate to the topic sentence of each paragraph and to the thesis of the essay?

Emphasis: Call attention to your important ideas. (See p. A-1 for page numbers.)

- Are ideas properly placed (especially near the beginning and end) for emphasis?
- Are important words and phrases repeated for emphasis?
- Are short sentences used among long ones to attract attention?

Support: Back up your controlling ideas with evidence and logic. (See p. A-1 for page numbers.)

- Is there adequate material—such as examples, details, quotations, and explanations—to support each topic sentence and thesis?
- Are the points of support placed in the best possible order?

Sentences: Write correct, effective sentences with structural variety. (See p. A-1 for page numbers.)

- Are the sentences varied in length and beginnings?
- Are the sentences varied in pattern (simple, compound, complex, and compound-complex)?

Editing with CGPS

To help you recall key features of correct writing (fundamentals or mechanics), as you repair your first draft through editing, the Brandon Guide offers an acronym: CGPS. Pronounced "see GPS" for easy memorization, CGPS provides reminders, or a checklist, for problems with **c**apitalization, **g**rammar, **p**unctuation, and **s**pelling. Discussed in detail in the Handbook, these features of editing need not be addressed one at a time or in a particular order, and going backward and forward for editing is just as important as going backward and forward with your revising. These elements of editing can be dealt with at any point during your writing, but most writers prefer to address them mainly during the final stages.

Capitalization: See p. A-1 for page numbers.

Capitalization, along with punctuation, makes it possible to see easily where sentences begin and end. Capitalization and lower case lettering can indicate whether nouns are simple or proper, whether something is a direction or a region, whether a phrase is just a phrase or a title. In short, good capitalization makes reading easier. Bad capitalization does the opposite. Often equally important, bad capitalization, after perhaps a bit of puzzlement by the reader, is recognized for what it is and brings unfavorable attention to the written statement.

Grammar: See p. A-1 for page numbers.

In the course you are now taking, knowledge of grammar can help you understand your English instructor's comments on your papers and help you make sound choices in your writing. It can also help you understand how language can be used in a variety of ways, freeing you to be more original in phrasing your sentences. In a broad sense, grammar overlaps with sentences in CLUESS for variety as it pertains to sentence patterns, sentence beginnings, and even sentence correctness for fragments, comma splices, and run-ons. For this CGPS sense, grammar will help you understand such aspects as subject and verb agreement, verb tense, pronoun case, proper modification, and parallel structure. Recognizing grammatical structures will often help you understand punctuation.

Punctuation: See p. A-1 for page numbers.

Good punctuation can make for easy reading. If you want to test that statement, try removing all punctuation from a passage and then try to read the passage swiftly. Punctuation is far more than decoration. It can change the meaning of sentences in many instances and, if wrong, can bring discredit to what you write and to you as an educated, thoughtful person. Punctuation can even be the basis for a lawsuit. For an author it can be enjoyable to use because it directs flow and establishes the rhythm of sentences.

Spelling: See p. A-1 for page numbers.

Spelling correctly makes your writing easier to read. The distraction of bad spelling can even contribute to the view that your thoughts are less profound than the thoughts of those who are good spellers, a view that is not necessarily true, but you still do not want anything to get in the way of your effective communication with others. Along with some simple rules, a list of the most commonly misspelled words appears in the Handbook.

Cyrus Norton wrote this first draft, marked it for revision, and then completed the final draft, which you read on pages 5–6. For simplification, only this draft is shown, although a typical paper might require several drafts, including one on which the author has done nothing but edit his or her revised writing.

Magic Johnson~~,~~ _an NBA Great_

(National Basketball Association)
Some NBA players are good because they
have a special talent.
~~are good~~ in one area~~, such as shooting,~~

~~passing, or rebounding.~~ Magic Johnson was _a_

NBA star   excellent   shooting, passing,
great because he was ~~good~~ in ~~all of those~~
rebounding, and leading
~~things and more.~~ As a shooter few have ~~been~~
ever equaled him
~~able to do what he could.~~ He could slam,

shovel, hook, and fire from three-point
                    —all with deadly accuracy   As for
ran~~/~~ge. ~~When it came to~~ free throws, he led

all NBA players in shooting percentage in
                While
1988-89. ~~Then,~~ he averaged more than twenty

points per game, he helped others become
with his passes   (the quarterback of basketball)
stars. As the point guard he was always near

                                _s_
the top in the league in a~~s~~sists and was

famous for his "no-look" passe~~s~~ _W_hich often
                                        its
surprised even his teammates with ~~their~~
When he wasn't shooting or passing, he was rebounding.
precision. A top rebounding guard is unusual,

but Magic, ~~standing~~ at six feet nine inches
                        _u_
tall, could bump sho~~l~~ders and jump with

anyone. These three qualities made him

probably the most spectacular triple-double

"Triple-double" means reaching two digits in scoring, assists, and rebounding.
threat of all time. Magic didn't need more

for greatness in the NBA, but he had more. He

was also an inspirational team leader with

his everlasting smile and boundless energy.

He   ed
Always believing in himself and his team.

When his team was down by a point and three

remained on the game clock   the fans
seconds were left, you always looked for

                                   They
Magic to get the ball. Then you watched as he

            he   he   he
dribbled once, faded, leaped, twisted, and

he | That was magic.
hooked one in from twenty feet! That was

Magic.

Exercise 1 Revising and Editing

Treat the following paragraph as your own rough draft, and mark it in the way Cyrus Norton marked his rough draft. First consider **c**oherence, **l**anguage, **u**nity, **e**mphasis, **s**upport, and **s**entences *(CLUESS). Then edit the paragraph, correcting fundamentals such as* **c**apitalization, **g**rammar, **p**unctuation, and **s**pelling *(CGPS).*

Delete Dress Codes

High school dress codes don't make any sense to me. I've heard all the reasons. Too many kids wear gang clothes and some get attacked or even killed. Parents have to put up too much money and even then the kids

without parents with deep pockets can't compete. And then
there are those that say kids behave bad if they dress
in a free spirit way. Let's take them one at a time.
As for the gang stuff, it's mainly how you act, not how
you look, and if the gang stuff is still a problem, then
just ban certain items of clothing. You don't have to go
to the extreames of uniforms, just change the attitude,
not the clothes. Then comes the money angle. Let the kid
get a part-time job if they want better clothes. The
behavior number is not what I can relate to. I mean, you
go to class and learn, and you do it the school way, but
the way you dress should have something to do with how
you want to express yourself. Do they want to turn out a
bunch of little robots that think the same way, behave
the same way, and yes with the dress code even look the
same way. Get real! If they'll cut us some slack with how
we dress, they'll get happier campers in the classroom.
Later better-citizens in society.

Exercise 2   Revising and Editing

*Mark the following rough draft for **c**oherence, **l**anguage, **u**nity, emphasis, **s**upport, and **s**entences (**CLUESS**). Then edit it, correcting
fundamentals such as **c**apitalization, **g**rammar, **p**unctuation, and
spelling (**CGPS**).*

Pain Unforgettable

One evening in 2008 while I was working the swing
shift at the General Tire Recapping Plant. I came up
with the greatest pain of my life because of a terible

accident. Raw rubber was heated up in a large tank. Pryor
to its being fed into an extruder. I was recapping large
off-road tires. The lowering platform was in the up
position the chain snapped. It sent the heavy platform
crashing down into the tank. This caused a huge wave of
steaming water to surge out of the tank. Unfortunately, I
was in its path the wave hit my back just above my waist.
The sudden pain shook me up. I could not move. My clothes
were steaming I freaked out. Co-workers ran to my aid and
striped the hot clothing from my body, taking skin as they
did. I lay face down on the plant floor, naked and shaking
for a long time. The paramedics came to pick me up. The
painful experience is still scary when I think about it.

Exercise 3 Revising and Editing

*Mark the following rough draft for **c**oherence, **l**anguage, **u**nity, **e**m-
phasis, **s**upport, and **s**entences (**CLUESS**). Then edit it, correcting
fundamentals such as **c**apitalization, **g**rammar, **p**unctuation, and
spelling (**CGPS**).*

                    If I Were a Traffic Cop

     Make me a traffic cop, and I'll crack down on
certain types of driver. First off are the drunks. I'd
zap them off the highways right off, and any cop would.
But what I'm really talking about is the jerks of the
highway. Near the top are the up-tight lane changers, for
example, this morning when I was driving to school, I saw
several. I could have carved at least a couple notches
in a vilation pad, and I wasn't even cranky. They cut off

people and force their way in, and leave behind upset and
hurt people. Then there's the left-turn bullies the ones
that keep moving out when the yellow turn to red. They
come in all ages and sexes, they can be young or old,
male or female. Yesterday, I saw this female in a pick-up
barrel right out into the teeth of a red light. She had
a baby on board. She had lead in her foot. She had evil
in her eye. She was hostile and self-centered. Taking
advantage of others. She knew that the facing traffic
would probably not pull out and risk a head-on crash.
The key word there is probably but many times people with
a green light do move out and colide with the left turn
bullies. Third, I'd sap the tailgaters. No one goes fast
enough for these guys. I'm not alone in this peeve. One
bumper sticker reads, "Stay back. I chew tobacky." And
James Bond sprayed oil on cars that chased him. Since
the first is dirty and the second is against the law, if
I had the clout of a Rambo-cop I'd just rack up a lot
of tailgater tickets. But there's a lot of road demons
out there. Maybe it's good I'm not a traffic cop, Rambo
or otherwise, cause traffic cops are suppose to inforce
hundreds of laws. I don't know if I'd have time cause
I have my own pet peeves in mind.

Exercise 4   Writing a Paragraph

Fill in the following two blanks to complete this topic sentence:
_____ *[person's name] is an excellent* _____ *[boss, coach, doctor,*
neighbor, parent, preacher, teacher, sibling]. Then use the topic sentence

to write a paragraph. Go through the complete writing process. Use one or more prewriting techniques (freewriting, brainstorming, listing, clustering, outlining), write a first draft, revise your draft as many times as necessary, edit your work, and write a final, polished paragraph.

In your drafts, you may rephrase the topic sentence as necessary. Using the paragraph on pages 6–7 in Chapter 1 (showing Magic Johnson as a shooter, passer, rebounder, and leader) as a model, divide your topic into whatever qualities make your subject an excellent example of whichever type of person you have chosen.

Writer's Guidelines at a Glance: Writing, Revising, and Editing

1. **Write the rough draft.** Referring to your outline for guidance and to your topic sentence for limits, write a first, or rough, draft. Do not get caught up in correcting and polishing your writing during this stage.

2. **Revise.** Mark and revise your rough draft, rewriting as many times as necessary to produce an effective paragraph. The main points of revision are contained in the acronym CLUESS, expressed here as questions.

   Coherence: Does the material flow smoothly from one idea to the next?

   Language: Are the words appropriate (with a consistent point of view) for the message, occasion, and audience?

   Unity: Are all the ideas related to and subordinate to the topic sentence?

   Emphasis: Have you used techniques such as repetition and placement of ideas to emphasize your main point(s)?

   Support: Have you provided material, such as examples, details, and reasoning, to back up, justify, or prove your topic sentence?

   Sentences: Have you written correct, effective sentences with varied structure?

3. **Edit.** Examine your work carefully. Look for problems in capitalization, grammar, punctuation, and spelling (CGPS).

3

Paragraphs
and Essays

⌒ Writing the Short Essay

The definition of a developmental paragraph gives us a framework for defining the essay: A **developmental paragraph** is a group of sentences, each with the function of supporting a single, main idea, which is contained in the topic sentence.

The key parts of a paragraph are the topic sentence (subject and focus), support (evidence and reasoning), and, often, the concluding sentence at the end. Now let's use that framework for an essay: An **essay** is a group of paragraphs, each with the function of stating or supporting a controlling idea called the thesis.

Following are the key parts of the essay:

Introduction: carries the thesis, which states the controlling idea—much like the topic sentence for a paragraph but on a larger scale—by giving the subject and focus
Development: support for the thesis
Conclusion: an appropriate ending—often a restatement of or a reflection on the thesis

Thus, considered structurally, the paragraph is frequently an essay in miniature. That does not mean that all paragraphs can expand into essays or that all essays can shrink into paragraphs. For college writing, however, a good understanding of the parallel between well-organized paragraphs and well-organized essays is useful. As you learn the properties of effective paragraphs—those with a strong topic sentence and strong support—you also learn how to organize an essay, if you just magnify the procedure.

32

The following diagram illustrates the parallel parts of outlines, paragraphs, and essays.

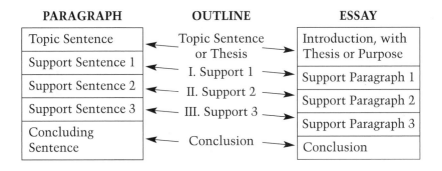

PARAGRAPH	OUTLINE	ESSAY
Topic Sentence	Topic Sentence or Thesis	Introduction, with Thesis or Purpose
Support Sentence 1	I. Support 1	
Support Sentence 2	II. Support 2	Support Paragraph 1
Support Sentence 3	III. Support 3	Support Paragraph 2
		Support Paragraph 3
Concluding Sentence	Conclusion	Conclusion

Of course, the parallel components are not exactly the same in a paragraph and an essay. The paragraph is shorter and requires much less development, and some paragraph topics simply couldn't be developed much more extensively to their advantage. But let's consider the ones that can. What happens? How do we proceed?

Introductory Paragraph

The topic-sentence idea is expanded to the introductory paragraph through elaboration: explanation, historical background, anecdote, quotation, or stress on the significance of an idea. Usually the introduction is three to six sentences long. If you say too much, your paper will be top-heavy. If you don't say enough, your readers will be confused. But a solid opening paragraph should

- introduce the subject through the thesis, or controlling idea.
- gain reader interest.
- move the reader into the middle paragraphs.
- avoid any statement of apology about your topic or your writing.
- avoid a needless change in point of view (first, second, third person)
- avoid beginning with a statement like "I am writing an essay about. . . ."

Middle Paragraphs

The middle paragraphs are similar to the paragraphs you have been writing. Each has its own unity based on the topic sentence, moves logically and coherently, and has adequate and appropriate development. The topic sentence is usually at the beginning of the paragraph in a college essay, regardless of the form. Although some essays are an expansion of a particular form of discourse and, therefore, use basically the same pattern for each paragraph, many essays combine the forms. For example, you might have one middle paragraph that gives examples, one that defines, and one that classifies. You may also have combinations within paragraphs. Nevertheless, the paragraphs are always related to the central idea and are presented in a logical arrangement. The coherence of the paragraphs can often be improved by the use of the same principles that you have applied within each paragraph: using sequence words such as *first, second,* and *third*; using transitional words such as *therefore, moreover*, and *for example*; and arranging material in chronological order, spatial order, or order of relative importance.

Concluding Paragraph

Like the introductory paragraph, the concluding paragraph is a special unit with a specific function. In the concluding paragraph, usually three to six sentences long, you end on a note of finality. The way you end depends on what you want to do. If you can't decide on how to end, try going back to your introduction and see what you said there. If you posed a question, the answer should be in the conclusion. If you laid out the framework for an exploration of the topic, then perhaps you will want to bring your discussion together with a summary statement. Or maybe a quotation, an anecdote, or a restatement of the thesis in slightly different words would be effective. Do not end with a complaint, an apology, or the introduction of a new topic or new support. And do not begin your conclusion with words such as "last but not least" or "in conclusion." Try for a fresh approach.

∼ Examining a Paragraph and an Essay

Student Writing

Here is the paragraph, followed by the essay on page 36.

Superman and Batman (paragraph)

Judy Urbina

**Topic
sentence
(subject,
focus)**   Both Superman and Batman are heroes, but only one is truly a superhero, and taking into

account their upbringing, motives, and criminal targets, that is Batman. Upbringing was not

I. Upbringing
A. Superman

gentle for either. Superman came from Krypton, a planet that was about to self-destruct. His parents sent him as a baby on a spaceship to Earth. There he would be adopted by an ordinary farm family. His adoptive parents named him Clark Kent and reared him well. In the same

B. Batman

generation, far away in Gotham, Bruce Wayne, the future Batman, was born to a contented, wealthy family. Tragically, his parents were killed in his presence during a mugging. He inherited the family wealth and was raised by his kindly butler. Those very different backgrounds provided Superman and Batman with powerful but

II. Motives
A. Superman

different motives for fighting crime. Superman was programmed in his space capsule to know about the forces of good and evil on Earth and to fight the bad people. Unlike Superman,

B. Batman

Batman learned from experience. Both have gone on to fight many bad people, but each one has a

III. Enemies
A. Superman

special enemy. For Superman, it is Lex Luthor, who has studied Superman and knows all about him, even his outstanding weakness—the mineral

B. Batman

Kryptonite. For Batman, it is the Joker, who, as a wicked teenager, was the mugger-murderer of Batman's parents. Many spectacular battles have ensued for both crime fighters, and one has reached the top in his profession. Superman offers overwhelming physical strength against crime, but Batman displays cunning and base passion. As he strikes fear in the hearts

Concluding
statement

of the wicked, he's not just winning; he is getting even. Most people would cheer Superman on. However, they would identify more with Batman, and he is the superhero.

Superman and Batman (essay)
Judy Urbina

1   During the Depression in the 1930s,
Superman and Batman were created as the first
big comic-book heroes. More than two thousand
similar but lesser characters were to follow.
Both Superman and Batman have been enormously
successful, but one seems to have more
personality and is probably closer to most of
us emotionally. Which hero wins out in this

Thesis struggle for our hearts and minds? Taking
(subject, into account their upbringing, motives, and
focus) criminal targets, one can argue that it is
Batman who is more credible.

2   Neither came originally from a home
I. Upbringing environment we are likely to identify with
A. Superman completely. Superman was conceived on the
planet Krypton by a highly intelligent
couple. His life was threatened because
Krypton was going to destruct. Superman's
parents bundled him up in a kiddie
spacecraft and launched him on a long
journey to Earth to save his life. He was
raised on a farm by Jonathan and Martha
Kent, who adopted him and grew to love
B. Batman him as their own. Batman, however, had an
upbringing which we can more easily imagine
as a complete pattern. Really Bruce Wayne
in disguise, Batman was left an orphan by
his parents, who were killed in a mugging
right in front of him. Fortunately for
Bruce Wayne, his parents were rich, and he
inherited millions when they died. He was
raised by his butler, unlike Superman, who
was nurtured by a conventional adoptive mom

and dad. Obviously the upbringing of these two heroes had a lot to do with the kind of heroes they grew up to be.

II. Motives 3   Both comic-book heroes had different motives for confronting killers and spoilers.

A. Superman   Superman instinctively knew he was sent to Earth to fight crime. When his birth parents shipped him off to Earth as an infant, they programmed the spacecraft to educate him on the ways of the Earthlings. Superman's adoptive parents reinforced those lessons by teaching him that he had to hide his powers and use them for the well-being of the human

B. Batman   race. To the contrary, Batman soon became a revenge-driven vigilante after his parents were killed in the mugging, so he decided to devote his life to fighting crime, with his butler as a domestic accomplice. To Batman no criminal is a good criminal. Although all of us citizens know we should not take the law into our own hands, nevertheless, we celebrate Superman and Batman as heroes, all the time identifying more with the guy in the fancy bat car.

III. Enemies 4   Like all superheroes, each of these two

A. Superman has an archenemy. Superman's archenemy is Lex Luthor, who has a brilliant criminal mind. Lex Luthor is always trying to destroy Superman. He knows everything about Superman, right down to his weakness—

B. Batman the mineral Kryptonite. Batman's main enemy is the Joker. As a teen, the Joker killed Batman's parents. Then Batman "accidentally" dropped the Joker into acid and permanently disfigured his face, so they are constantly getting into battles.

More people are able to relate to Batman because most of us at least think about vengeance if someone has done us wrong. Superman just wants to fight for "truth, justice, and the American way," all worthwhile values, but they're abstract.

Conclusion 5   Superman does not offer love or self-knowledge as keys to a perfect world. He offers only physical strength. Displaying more cunning and base passion, Batman preys on fears and insecurities of criminals as keys to a perfect world. He wants to keep the bad men and women intimidated and on the run. His presence in Gotham strikes fear in the hearts of the wicked. Neither crime fighter is much concerned about rehabilitation. Mainly they knock heads. But Batman seems to enjoy his work more than Superman because Batman's getting even. The fact that Batman fans are in touch with that source of satisfaction says as much about society as it does about Batman.

Exercise 1   Discussion and Critical Thinking

1. Are the characterizations consistent with the depictions of the characters in films you have seen? Explain.

2. Why is one character likely to be regarded as more admirable than the other? Explain.

3. How are the leading characters significantly defined by their enemies?

4. What is the point of this essay?

Exercise 2   Expanding a Paragraph into an Essay

The following paragraph could easily be expanded into an essay because the topic sentence and its related statements can be developed into an introduction; each of the main divisions (five) can be expanded into a separate paragraph; and the restated topic sentence can, with elaboration, become the concluding paragraph. Divide the following paragraph with the symbol ¶ and annotate it in the left-hand margin with the words Introduction, Support *(and numbers for the middle five paragraphs), and* Conclusion *to show the parts that would be developed further. The topic sentence has been marked for you.*

What Is a Gang?

Will Cusak

Topic sentence with related statements

The word *gang* is often used loosely to mean "a group of people who go around together," but that does not satisfy the concerns of law-enforcement people and sociologists. For these professionals, the definition of *gang* has five parts. These five parts combine to form a unit. First, a gang has to have a name. Some well-known gang names are Bloods, Crips, Hell's Angels, and Mexican Mafia. The second part of the definition is clothing or other identifying items, such as tattoos. The clothing may be of specific brands or colors, such as blue for Crips and red for Bloods. Members of the Aryan Brotherhood often have blue thunderbolt tattoos. A third component is rituals. They may involve such things as the use of handshakes, other body language or signing, and graffiti. A fourth is binding membership. A gang member is part of an organization, a kind of family, with obligations and codes of behavior to follow. Finally, a gang will be involved in some criminal behavior, something such as prostitution, drugs, thievery, or burglary. There are many different kinds of gangs—ethnic, regional, behavioral—but they all have these five characteristics.

〜 Topics for Short Essays

Many paragraph topics in this book can become topics for short essays. Look through the lists of Reading-Based Writing Topics, General Topics, Cross-Curricular Topics, and Career-Related Topics at the end of Chapters 6 through 15 to find ideas that can be expanded. Here are some ways to accomplish the expansion.

> **Narration:** Expand each part of the narrative form (situation, conflict, struggle, outcome, and meaning) into one or more paragraphs. Give the most emphasis to the struggle.
>
> **Description:** Expand each unit of descriptive detail into a paragraph. All paragraphs should support the dominant impression.
>
> **Exemplification:** Expand one example into an extended example or expand a group of examples into separate paragraphs. Each paragraph should support the main point.
>
> **Analysis by division:** Expand the discussion by treating each part of the unit in a separate paragraph.
>
> **Process analysis:** Expand the preparation and each step in the process into a separate paragraph.
>
> **Cause and effect:** Expand each cause or effect into a separate paragraph.
>
> **Classification:** Expand each class into a separate paragraph.
>
> **Comparison and contrast:** In the point-by-point pattern, expand each point into a separate paragraph. In the subject-by-subject pattern, first expand each subject into a separate paragraph. If you have sufficient material on each point, you can also expand each point into a separate paragraph.
>
> **Definition:** Expand each aspect of the definition (characteristics, examples, and comparative points) into a separate paragraph.
>
> **Argument:** Expand the refutation and each main division of support into a separate paragraph.

Of course, the statement that a paragraph is seldom made up of a single pattern also applies to the essay. Most essays have a combination of patterns, although one pattern may prevail and provide the main structure. Therefore, any topic selected from the end-of-chapter suggestions should be developed with an open mind about possibilities of using more than one pattern of development.

Writer's Guidelines at a Glance: Paragraphs and Essays

You do not usually set out to write an essay by first writing a paragraph. But the organization for the paragraph and the essay is often the same, and the writing process is also the same. You still proceed from prewriting to topic, to outline, to draft, to revising, to editing, to final paper. The difference is often only a matter of development and indentation.

1. The well-designed paragraph and the well-designed essay often have the same form.

   a. The **introduction** carries the thesis, which states the controlling idea—much like the topic sentence for a paragraph but on a larger scale.
   b. The development, or middle part, supplies evidence and reasoning—the **support**.
   c. The **conclusion** provides an appropriate ending—often a restatement of, or a reflection on, the thesis.

2. The following diagram shows the important relationships among the paragraph, outline, and essay.

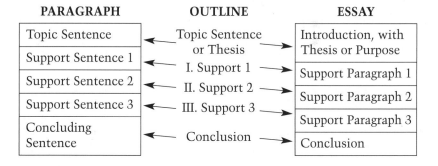

PARAGRAPH	OUTLINE	ESSAY
Topic Sentence	Topic Sentence or Thesis	Introduction, with Thesis or Purpose
Support Sentence 1	I. Support 1	Support Paragraph 1
Support Sentence 2	II. Support 2	Support Paragraph 2
Support Sentence 3	III. Support 3	Support Paragraph 3
Concluding Sentence	Conclusion	Conclusion

4

Reading Techniques

Reading-based writing is presented in this early chapter because all writing instruction in this book involves reading in some way. The abundant student and professional readings (more than thirty) were selected to stimulate thought and discussion, to provide content for writing, and to inform writing by strong examples of techniques and forms. Even reading-based writing has its own different forms, and reading itself has its own techniques. Here are five of the most common techniques for reading:

- Underlining
- Annotating
- Outlining
- Taking notes
- SQ3R—a systematic approach

Learning to use these techniques will help you move smoothly to the writing forms of reading-based writing that you will study in Chapter 5: summary, reaction, and two-part response.

∼ Underlining

One way to build concentration in reading is to develop a relationship with the reading material. Imagine you are reading a chapter of several pages and you decide to underline (highlighting functions in the same ways) text and write in the margins. Immediately, the underlining takes you out of the passive, television-watching frame of mind. You are involved. You are participating. It is now necessary for you to discriminate, to distinguish more important from less important ideas. Perhaps you have thought of underlining as a method designed only to help you with reviewing; that is, when you study the material the next time, you will not have to reread all the material. Instead, you can review only the most important, underlined

42

parts. However, even while you are underlining, you are benefiting from an imposed concentration because this procedure forces you to think, to focus. Consider the following guidelines for underlining:

1. Underline the main ideas in paragraphs. The most important statement, the topic sentence, is likely to be at the beginning of the paragraph.
2. Underline the support for those main ideas.
3. Underline answers to questions that you bring to the reading assignment. These questions may have come from the end of the chapter, from subheadings that you turn into questions, or from your independent concern about the topic.
4. Underline only the key words. You would seldom underline all the words in a sentence and almost never in a whole paragraph.

Does that fit your approach to underlining? Possibly not. Most students, in their enthusiasm to do a good job, overdo underlining.

Maybe you have had this experience: You start reading about something you have not encountered before. The idea seems important. You underline it. The next idea is equally fresh and significant. You underline it. A minute or two later, you have underlined the whole page, but you haven't accomplished anything.

The trick is how to figure out what to underline. You would seldom underline more than about 30 percent of a passage, although the amount would depend on your purpose and the nature of the material. Following the preceding four rules will be useful. Learning more about the principles of sentence, paragraph, and essay organization will also be helpful. These principles are presented in Chapters 1, 2, and 3.

~ Annotating

Annotating, a technique related to underlining, is writing in the margins. You can do it independently, although it usually appears in conjunction with underlining to mark the understanding and to extend the involvement.

Writing in the margins represents intense involvement because it makes you a writer. If you read material and write something in the margin as a reaction to it, then in a way you have begun a conversation with the author. The author has made a statement and you have responded. In fact, you may have added something to the text; therefore, for your purposes you have become a co-author or collaborator. The comments you make in the margin are of your own choosing according to your interests and the purpose you bring to the reading assignment. Your response in the margin may merely echo the author's ideas, it may question them critically, it may relate them to something else, or it may add to them.

In the following example, you can see how the reader has reinforced the underlining by commenting in the margin.

Women and Witchcraft

Mary Beth Norton

Salem witchcraft— broad interest

1   The Salem witchcraft crisis of 1692 to 1693, in which a small number of adolescent girls and young women accused hundreds of older women (and a few men) of having bewitched them, has fascinated Americans ever since. It has provided material for innumerable books, plays, movies, and television productions. To Americans of the twenty-first century the belief in witchcraft in the seventeenth-century colonies is difficult to explain or understand; perhaps that is why the Salem episode has attracted so much attention. For those interested in studying women's experiences, of course, witchcraft incidents are particularly intriguing. The vast majority of suspected witches were female, and so, too, were many of their accusers. Although colonial women rarely played a role on the public stage, in witchcraft cases they were the primary actors. What accounts for their prominence under these peculiar circumstances?

Why mostly women?

Historical/ cultural background

Without modern science

2   To answer that question, the Salem crisis must be placed into its proper historical and cultural context. People in the early modern world believed in witchcraft because it offered a rationale for events that otherwise seemed random and unfathomable. In the absence of modern scientific knowledge about such natural phenomena as storms and diseases, and clear explanations for accidents of various sorts, the evil actions of a witch could provide a ready answer to a person or community inquiring about the causes of a disaster.

Witch hunts   3   Therefore, witchcraft accusations—and
in Europe—   some large-scale witch hunts—were not uncom-
the extent   mon in Europe between the early fourteenth and
                       the late seventeenth centuries (1300 to 1700). In
                       short, the immigrants to the colonies came from
                       a culture in which belief in witchcraft was wide-
                       spread and in which accusations could result in
                       formal prosecutions and executions. Recent re-
                       search has demonstrated that the Salem incident,
                       although the largest and most important witch
                       hunt in New England, was just one of a number of
                       such episodes in the American colonies.

Question—   4   But why were witches women? Admit-
repeated   tedly, historians have not yet answered that
                       question entirely satisfactorily. Certain obser-
Answers: 1   vations can be made: women gave birth to new
2   life and seemed to have the potential to take
3   life away. In Western culture, women were seen
Women seen   as less rational than men, more linked to the
as "out of   natural world, in which magic held sway. Men,
their place"   who dominated European society, defined the
                       characteristics of a proper woman, who was
                       submissive and accepted a subordinate posi-
                       tion. The stereotypical witch, usually described
                       as an aggressive and threatening older woman,
                       represented the antithesis of that image. These
                       broad categories need further refinement, and
                       historians are currently looking closely at the
                       women who were accused of practicing witch-
                       craft to identify the crucial characteristics that
                       set them apart from their contemporaries and
                       made them a target for accusations.

—Mary Beth Norton, *Major Problems*
in American Women's History
(Boston: Houghton Mifflin), p. 113.

Exercise 1   Underlining and Annotating

Mark the following paragraphs with underlining and annotation.
Compare your marks with those of your classmates.

Buddha Taught Nonviolence

1   Buddha gave his first sermon to the five wisdom seekers who had been his companions. That sermon was a landmark in the history of world religions. Buddha taught the four main ideas that had come to him in his enlightenment, calling them the Four Noble Truths.

2   *First Noble Truth*: Everything in life is suffering and sorrow.

3   *Second Noble Truth*: The cause of all this pain is people's self-centered cravings and desires. People seek pleasure that cannot last and leads only to rebirth and more suffering.

4   *Third Noble Truth*: The way to end all pain is to end all desires.

5   *Fourth Noble Truth*: People can overcome their desires and attain enlightenment by following the Eightfold Path.

6   The Eightfold Path was like a staircase. According to Buddha, those who sought enlightenment had to master one step at a time. The steps of the Eightfold Path were right knowledge, right purpose, right speech, right action, right living, right effort, right mindfulness, and right meditation. By following the Eightfold Path, anyone could attain *nirvana* (nur-VAHN-uh), Buddha's word for release from pain and selfishness.

7   Buddha taught his followers to treat all living things (humans, animals, and even insects) with loving kindness. A devout Buddhist was not even supposed to swat a mosquito.

8   Buddhists and Hindus both sought to escape from the woes of this world, but their paths of escape were very different. Unlike traditional Hinduism, Buddhism did not require complex rituals. Moreover, Buddha taught in everyday language, not in the ancient Sanskrit language of the Vedas and the Upanishads, which most Indians in 500 BCE could no longer understand. Buddha's religion was also unique in its concern for all human beings—women as well as men, lowborn as well as highborn.

⌒ Outlining

Outlining can pertain to both reading and writing. Among the writing that will be suggested as assignments in this book are outlines, summaries, and reactions. In some instances, you may use all three forms after reading a passage. The three forms are also associated with reading and critical thinking in that they contribute to reading comprehension and use systematic and analytical thought. The reading below is followed by student Leon Batista's outline. Note the parallel structure in his outline.

The Roman Toga

1   Practicality has never been a requirement of fashion. The Roman toga was an uncomfortable garment. It was hot in summer, cold in winter, and clumsy for just about any activity but standing still. The toga was, however, practical in one way: It was easy to make, since it involved no sewing. Not even a buttonhole was needed. An adult's toga was basically a large wool blanket measuring about 18 by 7 feet. It was draped around the body in a variety of ways without the use of buttons or pins.

2   In the early days of the Roman republic, both women and men wore togas. Women eventually wore more dresslike garments, called *stolas*, with separate shawls. For men, however, the toga remained in fashion with very little change.

3   Soon after the republic was formed, the toga became a symbol of Roman citizenship. Different styles of togas indicated a male citizen's place in society. For example, a young boy would wear a white toga with a narrow purple band along the border. When his family decided he was ready for adult responsibilities, he would don a pure white toga. On that day, usually when he was about 16, his family would take him to the Forum, where he would register as a full citizen. For the rest of his life, he would wear a toga at the theater, in court, for religious ceremonies, and on any formal occasion. At his funeral his body would be wrapped in a toga to mark him, even in death, as a Roman citizen.

—Steven L. Jantzen, *World History: Perspectives on the Past*
(Boston: Houghton Mifflin), pp. 79–80.

I. Practicality

  A. Not practical
    1. Hot in summer
    2. Cold in winter
    3. Clumsy

  B. Practical
    1. Easy to make
    2. Easy to put on and take off

II. Fashion in Roman republic

   A. Worn by men and women
      1. Changes little with men
      2. Alternates with stolas and shawls for women

   B. Symbol of citizenship
      1. One style for young male
      2. Another style for adult male
         a. Presented at point of adulthood
         b. Worn on all occasions

⌒ Taking Notes

Taking notes for reading-based writing in this book should be little more than marking and annotating passages in reading selections and jotting down the useful points for support in your outline as you organize your summary or reaction. While writing, you will use those notes for support as you refer directly to what you have read and you will use some quotations from the reading. You will also give credit to the source you are reading, and—if your instructor requires you to do so—you will use documentation of the approved style (usually MLA or APA), including page numbers and identification of your source(s) for those ideas and words you borrow.

    Here is an example of how you can place notes inside outlines. It is an excerpt from student Alex Mylonas's reading-based reaction to the short story "The Use of Force" by William Carlos Williams. During his first reading, Alex underlined and annotated freely; then later he selected phrases as support in his outline, which he submitted with a long paragraph assignment.

II. The inner conflict

   A. Doctor versus himself
      1. Wants to be professional
      2. Loses self-control
         "attractive little thing," p. 333
         "damned little brat," p. 333
      3. Loses sight of objective
         "got beyond reason," p. 334

   B. Emotional (brutal) side wins
         "It was a pleasure to attack her," p. 335
         "blind fury," p. 335

〜 SQ3R—A Systematic Approach

Proven to be effective in increasing reading efficiency, **SQ3R** is a comprehensive formula that can be altered to fit different purposes for different kinds of reading. As the name suggests, **SQ3R** consists of five stages: survey, question, read, recall, and review.

Survey

The first stage, the *survey*, is reading by skimming, or semi-reading, because it involves much skipping. You can easily modify it for speed reading. It is designed to give an overview; you survey to find the main ideas. For the typical essay or book chapter, this is the procedure:

1. Read the title and any background material to the work.
2. Read the entire first paragraph for the introduction, to discover what the author is attempting to say.
3. Read the subheadings (phrases indented and printed on a separate line in bold-faced or italic print). If there are no subheadings, read the first sentence of each paragraph. These elements should give you the main points of development.
4. Look at the illustrations.
5. Read the entire last paragraph or the concluding section labeled "summary." This conclusion should show what the author believes he or she has presented.
6. Read the questions, if any, at the end of the passage.

Question

Working with questions changes you from a passive into an active reader because then you are equipped with a purpose, you know what to look for. Questions may come from the end of the chapter, from the instructor, or from you yourself, as you reflect on the ideas generated by your survey.

Read

Naturally, this is the most important stage. The reading will proceed according to your purpose and the nature of the material. It may involve underlining and writing in margins. It may include intense interpretation. It certainly will include a thoughtful consideration of main ideas and support. The result will include answers to the questions proposed in the second stage.

Recall

Periodically, you should pause and attempt to recollect what you have read. *If you can summarize the material, you can proceed.* If you cannot, then reread the material.

Review

Review is to the chapter what recall is to two or three pages. At the end of the chapter, you should be able to provide the answers to the questions as well as recount other important points in the material.

The SQ3R approach offers you several benefits: *The survey provides an overview;* therefore, you will know where you are going. One section may be more understandable if you see it in the context of the whole piece. *The questions provide purpose. The recall and review stages provide tentative and final review.* The actual reading, then, is done within the context of a plan, a plan that may seem to add a bit of time to the reading process. However, all studies made on this method have shown that SQ3R saves time and results in more effective reading.

This system works best with longer pieces of material such as longer essays and book chapters. Obviously, you would not want or need to apply SQ3R to a paragraph, a short story, or a simple poem. Modification of this technique to fit the purpose of the reading and the nature of the material is exceedingly important.

When you are ready to read the next chapter of this text or when you read your next chapter-length assignment in another book, try using SQ3R.

Writer's Guidelines at a Glance: Reading Techniques

1. Underlining (or highlighting) helps you to read with discrimination and focus.

   - Underline the main ideas in paragraphs.
   - Underline the support for those ideas.
   - Underline answers to questions that you bring to the reading assignment.
   - Underline only the key words.

2. Annotating enables you to actively engage the reading material.
   - Number parts if appropriate.
   - Make comments according to your interests and needs.
3. Outlining the passages you read sheds light on the relationship of ideas, including the major divisions of the passage and their relative importance.
4. Taking notes will provide you with support when you write your reading-based paragraph or essay.
5. SQ3R—survey, question, read, recall, review—is a comprehensive system that works well when reading essays and chapters.

5

Reading-Based Writing

~ Reading-Based Writing Forms

For instruction in this book, reading-based writing comes in three forms: summary, reaction, and two-part response. In writing a summary, you use mostly your own words to restate the main ideas in what you have read. In writing a reaction, you comment critically on what you have read, while giving credit for the ideas and words you borrow. Then, in composing a two-part response, you write both a summary and a reaction, but you separate them to show your instructors that you know the difference between the two forms.

Writing a Summary

A summary is a rewritten, shortened version of a piece of writing in which you use your own wording to express the main ideas. Learning to summarize effectively will help you in many ways. Summary writing reinforces comprehension skills in reading. It requires you to discriminate among the ideas in the target reading passage. A summary is often written in the form of a well-designed paragraph. Frequently, summaries are used in collecting material for research papers and in writing conclusions to essays.

The following rules will guide you in writing effective summaries.

1. Cite both the author and the title of the text.
2. Reduce the length of the original by about two-thirds, although the exact reduction will vary depending on the content of the original.
3. Concentrate on the main ideas and include details only infrequently.
4. Change the original wording without changing the idea.

5. Do not evaluate the content or give an opinion in any way (even if you see an error in logic or fact).
6. Do not add ideas (even if you have an abundance of related information).
7. Do not include any personal comments (that is, do not use *I*, referring to self).
8. Use quotations only infrequently. (If you do use quotations, enclose them in quotation marks.)
9. Use author tags ("says York," "according to York," or "the author explains") to remind the reader that you are summarizing the material of another writer.
10. Begin with the main idea (as you usually do in middle paragraphs) and cover the main points in an organized fashion while using complete sentences.

The following is a summary of "The Roman Toga," written by Leon Batista, the student who prepared the sample outline on pages 47–48 in Chapter 4. When first reading the material, he had underlined key parts and written comments and echo phrases in the margin. Then he wrote his outline. Finally, referring to both the marked passage and the outline, Batista wrote this summary. Had he not been assigned to write the outline, he might have done so anyway, as preparation for writing his summary.

Summary of "The Roman Toga"
by Steven L. Jantzen

According to Steven Jantzen in *World History: Perspectives on the Past*, the toga was the main form of dress for citizens of the Roman republic, despite its being "hot in summer, cold in winter, and clumsy" to wear. Perhaps the Romans appreciated the simplicity of wearing a piece of woolen cloth about eighteen by seven feet "without the use of buttons or pins." Jantzen explains that the women also wore another garment similar to a dress called the *stola*, but Roman male citizens were likely to wear only the toga—white with a purple edge for the young and solid white for the adult. This apparel was worn from childhood to death.

Exercise 1   Evaluating a Summary

*Compare the following summary with the original passage (see
chapter 4, p. 47)and with the student summary you just read. Then
mark the instances of poor summary writing by underlining and by
using rule numbers from the preceding list.*

Summary About One of My Favorite Garments

For citizens of the Roman republic, the toga was the main
form of dress, despite its being hot in summer, cold in winter,
and clumsy to wear. Frankly, I don't see why a bright bunch
of people like the Romans couldn't have come up with a better design. Perhaps the Romans appreciated the simplicity of
wearing a piece of woolen cloth about eighteen by seven feet
without buttons or pins, but I've read elsewhere that the togas
were sometimes stolen at the public baths. The women also
wore another garment similar to a dress called the *stola*, but the
Roman male citizen was likely to wear only the toga—white
with a purple edge for the young and solid white for the adult. For
the rest of his life, he would wear a toga at the theater, in court,
for religious ceremonies, and on any formal occasion. At his
funeral, his body would be wrapped in a toga to mark him, even
in death, as a Roman citizen.

The three paragraphs in the following two sections are further examples of reading-based writing: the reaction and the two-part
response.

Writing a Reaction

A reaction concentrates on the content in a reading selection or selections. It includes personal experience and other information only
to explain, validate, or challenge the ideas in that content.

In the following reaction, student Shanelle Watson takes a
basic idea from the original passage (see chapter 4, p. 47) and finds
historical parallels. She begins and ends her paragraph with references to the content of the reading selection.

Sticks and Stones
Shanelle Watson

Reading "Women and Witchcraft" by Mary Beth Norton reminded me of a long line of indignities against women. If something goes wrong and women can be blamed, they are. For centuries if a woman did not have babies, it was said *she* could not, although the man was just as likely as the woman to be the cause of her childlessness. If, heaven forbid, the woman kept having female babies, that woman, it was said, couldn't produce a male. Yet we know now that it is the male who determines the sex of the child. If the child was not bright, as recently as a hundred years ago some doctors said it was because the woman was reading during pregnancy and took away the brain power from the fetus. As a result, many women were not allowed to open a book during pregnancy. Of course, because it was believed that women were so weak, husbands were allowed to beat their wives, but according to English law, the stick could be no thicker than the man's thumb, hence "the rule of thumb." Even voting was argued against by some who said that the typical woman, controlled by emotions, would allow her husband to tell her how to vote, and each married man would then have two votes. It is no wonder that three hundred years ago men looked around and, finding many misfortunes, decided that women were the culprits and should be punished. Sticks were not enough. It was time for stones.

Writing a Two-Part Response

As you have seen, the reaction includes an idea or ideas from a reading or is written with the assumption that readers have read the original piece. However, your instructor may prefer that you separate the forms and present a clear, concise summary followed by another type of reading-based writing. This format is especially

useful for critical reactions or problem-solving assignments because it requires you to understand and repeat another's views or
experiences before responding. The two-part response also helps you
avoid the common problem of writing only a summary of the text
when your instructor wants you to both summarize and evaluate
or to otherwise react. When writing a summary and a critical reply
to a reading assignment, be sure you know whether your instructor
wants you to separate your summary from your reaction.

The following reading-based writing first summarizes and then,
in a separate paragraph of reaction, analyzes, evaluates, and inter-
prets the original passage.

"Women and Witchcraft" by Mary Beth Norton:

A Summary and a Reaction

Jeanne Garcia

Part 1: Summary

Americans have long been fascinated by the Salem
witchcraft plight in 1692 to 1693. One perplexing
factor is that most of the people accused and many who
blamed them were women. In "Women and Witchcraft," Mary
Beth Norton says the whole issue should be placed in a
historical context. In those times, much was unknown
about the causes of disasters and illnesses, and the
people came to believe that these things could be
attributed to evil supernatural forces. Consequently,
from about 1300 to 1700 "witch hunts" occurred, and
Salem was just one of the locations. Historians are not
certain about why women were often victims and accusers.
They may have been involved because they had the power to
produce life and, therefore, maybe had "the potential to
take life away." Women were thought to be more emotional
than rational and even connected to nature, as in magic.
Moreover, the stereotypical witch was characterized as
a mature, assertive woman, unlike the "proper woman" of
the time "who was submissive and accepted a subordinate
position." Norton says that historians now seek to

discover the precise causes that made assertive women the victims of persecution as witches.

Part 2: Reaction

The "witchcraft crisis of 1692 to 1693," which Mary Beth Norton discusses in "Women and Witchcraft," is not so surprising to some of us who look back after three hundred years at the way some men treat some women. One does not have to read between Norton's lines. She makes it clear that "usually" the people were "aggressive and threatening older women." The charges came mainly from adolescent girls and young women, but the power structure was adult men. Out of ignorance, the men, often with female accomplices, were looking around to find reasons for the misfortunes—bad weather, diseases, and accidents—that their society faced. It is a fact that if people are foolish and desperate enough to look for witches, they are foolish and desperate enough to find them. And they did: They found mainly a few old women who did not know their place, individuals of a gender associated with the emotions. If these women had been meek and mild, if they had been properly submissive to the menfolk, and if they had still been young and sexy, they would not have been vulnerable. But they were what they were—mature and relatively independent women, who seemed to be different— and that made them witches to those who were said not to be emotionally based—the men.

∿ Kinds of Support for Reading-Based Writing

In your reading-based writing assignments, you are likely to use three methods in developing your ideas: explanations, direct references to the reading selection, and quotations from the reading selection.

- Your explanations will often be expressed in patterns, such as causes and effects, comparison and contrast, definition, or exemplification. These forms are presented in depth and related to reading-based writing in Chapters 6 through 15. Your discussion of personal experience will be used only to explain, validate, or challenge ideas from the reading selection.
- Your references will point your reader(s) directly toward original ideas in sources. The more specific the references, the more helpful they will be to your readers.
- Your quotations will be words borrowed from sources and credited to those sources. You will use quotation marks around those words, which will appear as sentences or as partial sentences blended with your own words.

∼ Basic Formal Documentation in Reading-Based Writing

Borrowing words or ideas without giving credit to the originator is called plagiarism and is not acceptable scholarship, regardless of whether it is intentional. To help you in learning to give credit accurately, your instructor may ask you to document your reading-based writing formally, even though the text is readily available and assigned. Formal documentation means you must indicate the location of all the original ideas you have borrowed, even if you have changed the words.

Citations

Documenting sources for reading-based writing should be done with care. This book uses a system called MLA (Modern Language Association) Style on a search engine such as Google. The *At a Glance* Student Companion Site also provides free instruction for the MLA form at www.cengage.brain.com. Primarily, you need to remember that when using material from a source you must give enough information so that the reader will recognize it or be able to find it in its original context. Here are the most common principles of documentation that can be used for textbook or other restricted sources, whether it is quoted, paraphrased (restated), or summarized.

If you use the author's name in introducing a quotation, then usually give only the page number.

EXAMPLE: Suzanne Britt says that "neat people are bums and clods at heart" (255).

If you use the author's name in introducing a borrowed idea, then usually give only the page number.

EXAMPLE: Suzanne Britt believes that neat people are weak in character (255).

If you do not use the author's name to introduce a quotation or an idea, then usually give both the author's name and the page number.

EXAMPLE: Music often helps Alzheimer's patients think more clearly (Weiss 112).

Works Cited

Work(s) Cited lists the sources used, meaning those that appear in citations, as shown in the previous section. Each kind of publication has its own order of parts and punctuation.

Here is an example of a Work Cited entry pertaining to a student writing. It is "A Work in an Anthology" (covered in the *At a Glance* Student Companion Site). Note the punctuation between parts and the order of those parts: author's name (last, first), title of composition (quotation marks for a short work; italics for a long work), editor(s) of the anthology, name of the anthology, edition if there is one, place of publication, publisher, date of publication, pages on which the selection appears, and medium of publication.

Work Cited

Ortiz, Charles C. "Not Invulnerable." *Sentences, Paragraphs, and Beyond: With Integrated Readings*. Ed. Lee Brandon and Kelly Brandon. 6th ed. Boston: Cengage, 2011. 325–26. Print.

～ Example of Reading-Based Writing

Student Reading-Based Paragraph (extracted from an essay)

Struggling Against Silence

Lydia Hsiao

Student Lydia Hsiao was asked to read and then write a reading-based reaction to a reading selection taken from Maxine Hong Kingston's The Woman Warrior. *This paragraph taken from Hsiao's short essay illustrates how to document sources.*

Maxine Hong Kingston and I came from a strict Chinese background and were taught that "a ready tongue is an evil" (Kingston 252). We were also taught to keep to ourselves. We were never taught to communicate with those outside our culture. This background may have caused my self-consciousness and my paralyzing fear of being embarrassed. During my first year in the United States, I was constantly teased about my Chinese accent. If I mispronounced a word during class, I could not help but be disgusted by my own mistakes, causing me even greater embarrassment. Kingston says, "[They] scare the voice away" (254). The result was that, like Kingston, my potential was for years undiscovered. In the same way Kingston allowed silence to "[paint] layers of black over [her life]" (254), silence continued to create a thicker darkness in my life. It first embarrassed me; then it soon robbed me of my self-esteem. As Kingston says, "[Talking] takes up that day's courage" (252). It was almost as if silence was more than a curtain. It seemed to grow its own body and walk beside me. That silence became my sinister friend, taking advantage of my willingness to accept this cruel school life, tricking me into believing that home was the only place I could find my voice. The monster silence kept me quiet.

Work Cited

Kingston, Maxine Hong. "Silence." *Rereading America*. Ed. Gary Colombo, Robert Cullan, and Bonnie Lisle. New York: Bedford/St. Martin's, 1998. 252-55. Print.

⌒ Essay for Discussion and Writing

The following essay by a student demonstrates many of the elements of good writing that we have been exploring. To help you evaluate and write in response to the selection, it is underlined and annotated. It is accompanied, at the end of the essay, by a set of discussion and critical-thinking questions and then by several reading-based writing suggestions. Take a look at the questions in Exercise 2 and the writing suggestions in Exercise 3 before you read the essay to help you focus your reading.

Student Writing

Everyone Pays the Price
Hadley McGraw

Sitting in a college classroom, Hadley McGraw doesn't remind one of the stereotypical gang member. Apparently tattoo- and puncture-free, she is fair-skinned, well-groomed, and soft-spoken. She does her homework, contributes to class discussion, and writes well. So much for stereotypes!

1   It is ten o'clock and time for me to start my day. I put an X on my calendar to signify that another twenty-four hours has passed. I now have one hundred and nine days until Martin, my boyfriend, comes home. He has been in jail for the last year. I guess you could say I was not surprised by his sentence. This is not the first time, and I am afraid it will not be the last. Eighteen months of our three-and-a-half-year relationship, he has spent in correctional institutions. Martin is a gang member. He has **Thesis** been a gang member for nine years now. Gang membership of a loved one affects everyone around that person. Three-and-a-half years later I live each day in fear and grief.

Topic 2   I guess what attracted me to Martin at **sentence** first was his bad-boy image and his carefree way of life. He was good looking and well known. He was tough and exciting. I, however, was good and obedient. I had been told often that I was pretty. I made good grades and came from a good home. My parents, still married and drug-free, lived comfortably

Causes

in a middle-class neighborhood. Martin, on
the contrary, came from a broken home. His
parents hated each other. His father was a
cold, heartless man, and his mother was a
"flakey" drug addict. His uncles and cousins
were all members of a very large gang that
"controlled" an area where he lived. Soon he
too was a gang member.

3   Martin quit school when he was a
freshman and spent his days on a street
corner drinking Olde English forty-ouncers.
Soon I was joining him. I began ditching
school to hang out. In no time, I was a
gang member myself and, as I look back,

Effects

I see what an awful person I became. We used
drugs all day and all night. I did not care
about anything and neither did he. I left
home and devastated my family and lost my
friends. I didn't care because I had a new
family and new friends. Martin spent his
nights committing crimes and dealing drugs.
I was by his side, carrying his gun. The
drugs made him irritable and violent, and
small disagreements turned into huge battles
between us. Jail sentences made him angrier
and closer to his gang. Each day Martin
became farther from me. Life was a nonstop
party with his homeboys, and I was his
woman. It was exciting and risky. It was
also self-destructive.

Topic
sentence

4   My breaking point was one year ago.
Martin and I were at a party. Everyone was
drinking and joking. Oldies were playing and
a noisy, wild game of poker was taking place.
Suddenly a car was approaching us rapidly.
Martin told me to run and hide, so I did.

The homeboys began reaching for their guns. I heard five gunshots before the car drove away. I ran to the front of the house where Martin's cousin lay bleeding. I tried to wake him, speak to him. He wasn't responding. I screamed for an ambulance. Finally Martin appeared from behind a car and ran inside to call 911. When the ambulance arrived,

Effects I was hysterical and covered in blood. They took Martin's cousin to the hospital where he was pronounced dead. Because of the gunshot wounds, the funeral was a closed-casket affair and very hard on everyone. It made Martin stronger, meaner, and colder, and it made me wiser. Martin was out committing crimes again; two months later, he would be jailed again.

5   It is hard for me to imagine what I did to myself, knowing that any day I could have died senselessly. It is even harder for me to accept the fact that my boyfriend would die for a dirty, trashy street gang but not

Topic for me. This last year I have been moving
sentence back to the right track. I have gotten sober, started college, and returned home. I have nightmares about things I have seen and things I have done. I struggle every day to stay sober, to do the right thing. I am doing

Effects a lot of thinking. I live each day in fear for Martin's safety as well as my own. I fear for our future in a society that does not understand us. I count down the days until Martin can see the sunlight. I pray every day that this time will be the last time he goes to jail. I pray Martin will trade his gun for me, even get an education. I cry every night and try to live every day.

Exercise 2   Discussion and Critical Thinking

1. Why did McGraw become associated with Martin and finally become a gang member?

2. Did she have deeper reasons for dropping out of mainstream, middle-class society and joining a gang? Explain.

3. What were the effects on McGraw's life and the lives of those who were close to her?

4. What happened before the killing to set the stage for McGraw's change?

5. To what extent has McGraw changed?

6. Why doesn't she leave Martin? Discuss.

7. What is your reaction to the statement "I fear for our future in a society that does not understand us" (paragraph 5)?

Exercise 3   Suggestions for Reading-Based Writing

On separate paper, complete one of the following reading-based responses. Use references and quotations in reactions.

1. Write a summary of McGraw's essay.

2. Write a two-part response to McGraw's essay composed of labeled summary and reaction parts.

3. Write a reaction in which you examine each part of McGraw's experience and discuss the relationship of the parts. Concentrate on the stages of her changes for bad and good. As you emphasize stages, resist any temptation to write only a summary. Another

approach would be to imagine that McGraw has written this essay to you, and now you are writing a paragraph of advice to her. Direct your advice to her through what she has written, using references and quotations.

Writer's Guidelines at a Glance: Reading-Based Writing

1. Summarizing helps you concentrate on main ideas. A summary

   - cites the author and title of the text.
   - is usually shorter than the original by about two-thirds, although the exact reduction will vary depending on the content of the original.
   - concentrates on the main ideas and includes details only infrequently.
   - changes the original wording without changing the idea.
   - does not evaluate the content or give an opinion in any way (even if the original contains an error in logic or fact).
   - does not add ideas (even if the writer of the summary has an abundance of related information).
   - does not include any personal comments by the writer of the summary (therefore, no use of *I*, referring to self).
   - seldom contains quotations (although, if it does, only with quotation marks).
   - includes some author tags ("says York," "according to York," or "the author explains") to remind the reader(s) that it is a summary of the material of another writer.
   - begins with the main idea and covers the main points in an organized fashion while using complete sentences.

2. Two other types of reading-based writing are

   - the reaction, which shows how the reading relates to you, your experiences, and your attitudes, and, also, is often a critique of the worth and logic of the piece.
   - the two-part response, which includes a summary and a reaction that are separate.

3. Most ideas in reading-based writing are developed in one or more of these three ways:

   - explanations
   - direct references
   - quotations

4. Documenting is giving credit to borrowed ideas and words.
5. Reading-based writing requires you to read a source and to use it as a model of form and treatment of an idea.
6. Write and revise.

   - Write and then revise your paragraph or essay as many times as necessary for coherence, language (usage, tone, and diction), unity, emphasis, support, and sentences (**CLUESS**). Read your work aloud to hear and correct any grammatical errors or awkward-sounding sentences.
   - Edit any problems in fundamentals, such as capitalization, grammar, punctuation, and spelling (**CGPS**).

7. Record your strengths and needs on the Self-Evaluation Chart just inside the front cover of this book, or go to the Student Companion Site at www.cengagebrain.com and print out an enlarged chart.

6

Narration: Moving Through Time

∼ Writing Paragraphs of Narration

In our everyday lives, we tell stories and invite other people to do so by asking questions such as "What happened at work today?" and "What did you do last weekend?" We are disappointed when the answer is "Nothing much." We may be equally disappointed when a person doesn't give us enough details or gives us too many and spoils the effect. After all, we are interested in people's stories and in the people who tell them. We like narratives.

What is a narrative? A **narrative** is an account of an incident or a series of incidents that make up a complete and significant action. A narrative can be as short as a joke, as long as a novel, or anything in between, including a single paragraph. Each narrative has five properties: situation, conflict, struggle, outcome, and meaning.

Situation

Situation is the background for the action. The situation may be described only briefly, or it may even be implied. ("To celebrate my seventeenth birthday, I went to the Department of Motor Vehicles to take my practical test for my driver's license.")

Conflict

Conflict is friction, such as a problem in the surroundings, with another person(s), or within the individual. The conflict, which is at the heart of each story, produces struggle. ("It was raining and my appointment was the last one of the day. The examiner was a serious, weary-looking man who reminded me of a bad boss I once had, and I was nervous.")

Struggle

Struggle, which need not be physical, is the manner of dealing with the conflict. The struggle adds action or engagement and generates the plot. ("After grinding on the ignition because the engine was already on, I had trouble finding the windshield wiper control. Next I forgot to signal until after I had pulled away from the curb. As we crept slowly down the rain-glazed street, the examiner told me to take the emergency brake off. All the while I listened to his pen scratching on his clipboard. 'Pull over and park,' he said solemnly.")

Outcome

Outcome is the result of the struggle. ("After I parked the car, the examiner told me to relax, and then he talked to me about school. When we continued, somehow I didn't make any errors, and I got my license.")

Meaning

Meaning is the significance of the story, which may be deeply philosophical or simple, stated or implied. ("Calmness promotes calmness.") Most narratives written as college assignments have an expository purpose (that is, they explain a specified idea). Often the narrative will be merely an extended example. Therefore, the meaning of the narrative is exceedingly important and should be clear, whether it is stated or implied.

These five properties are present in some way in all the many forms of the narrative. They are often enhanced by the use of various devices such as the following:

- **Description** (the use of specific details to advance action, with images to make readers see, smell, taste, hear, and feel)

  the *rain-glazed street*

  listened to his *pen scratching*

- **Dialogue** (the exact words of the speakers, enclosed in quotation marks)

  "*Pull over and park*," he said solemnly.

Transitional Words

Consider using the following transitional words to improve coherence by connecting ideas with ideas, sentences with sentences, and paragraphs with paragraphs:

- **FOR NARRATION   Time:** *after, before, later, earlier, initially, soon, recently, next, today, tomorrow, yesterday, now, then, until, currently, when, finally, not long after, immediately, (at) first, (at) last, third, previously, in the meantime, meanwhile*

- **FOR DESCRIPTION AS PART OF NARRATION   Place:** *above, over, under, below, nearby, near, across, beyond, among, to the right, to the left, in the background, in the foreground, further, beside, opposite, within sight, out of sight*

∼ Practicing Patterns of Narration

Exercise 1   Completing Patterns

Fill in the blanks to complete each narrative pattern.

1. Lost and Found Surprise

   (situation)   I. Person taking store money deposit bag to bank

   (conflict)   II. Person loses bag

   (struggle)   III. _____

   (outcome)   IV. _____

   (meaning)   V. _____

2. Good Samaritan Appears

   (situation)   I. Driver with flat tire, dead of night

   (conflict)   II. No spare tire

   (struggle)   III. _____

   (outcome)   IV. _____

   (meaning)   V. _____

～ Examining Paragraphs of Narration

Student Writing

King of Klutziness

Joel Bailey

We begin with a humorous paragraph by student writer Joel Bailey, who gives an account of his clumsiness as a worker in a fast-food establishment.

Topic sentence   It was my first task of what would be a memorable day at work in Carl's Jr., a

Place   fast-food place by <u>Universal Studios</u> near Hollywood. I was assigned to the front

Situation   counter because another worker was late.

Time   There I was at <u>noon</u>, the busiest time of the day, with no training, scared, and nervous. In the beginning, things went well. Orders were routine, and I filled them and made

Transition   change. <u>As time passed</u>, the lines got short, and I was still doing great because, after all, the job didn't require the mentality of a rocket scientist. Several counter people left their registers to help out in back. <u>Then</u> a lot of people came in at one time.

Transition Conflict   Only two of us were taking orders. I was nervous. I served three persons, hardly looking up as I punched the keys, called out orders, and made change. <u>After</u> barely

Transition Image: sound   glancing at the next person, <u>I heard his voice</u> ordering, a familiar voice. It was Alex Benson, a reporter for a TV channel I frequently watched. I repeated his order to him so that it would be perfect, and I took his money. <u>After</u> I gave him his change, he

Transition Struggle   stared at the receipt and said with more than a touch of irritation, <u>"You made a mistake.</u>

Dialogue	You charged me for two chicken burgers." I apologized and gave him a refund. "What about the tax," he growled. "You didn't refund the tax." I was really getting nervous. He always laughed and smiled on TV. I gave him the tax money. I grabbed someone else's chicken order just so I could give him quick service, but when I handed him the tray, my hand slipped and I spilled his Coke on his trousers.
Outcome	Quickly I grabbed a napkin and ran around the counter and wiped at the Coke stain.
Image: sight	Unfortunately the napkin I grabbed had catsup
Transition	on it. Now I had added a condiment to the Coke stain. By that time I might as well have salted and peppered him. Beyond anger,
Meaning	and looking at me wildly, he fled with his tray to a distant booth and sat with his back to the wall. I decided not to ask for an autograph.

Yearning for Love
Chantra Shastri

Having lived in the United States for five years, Chantra Shastri asks for freedom—freedom to make a choice in marriage, a choice based on love.

	I need not go beyond myself to find examples of love, at least the yearning for love. My home is now America, but I have not left India far behind. There, in ways still
Situation	cherished by my traditional family, freedom is based on gender, and I am a female. My parents expect women to cook, clean, and
Conflict	nurture. My parents expect me to marry the man of their choice, although my brother will have the freedom to choose his own mate.

Struggle

If I disobey, I will no longer be recognized by my parents. It is easy to give in to such a custom; it is difficult to disobey. My parents have always believed as they do. I cannot change them, nor do I want to, but I wish they would accept my difference in

Transition (focus within a narration)

this different country. I think my mother understands. <u>Last week</u>, I saw her crying while she ironed our clothes. When I asked her why she was crying, she wiped the warm tears off her thin, soft cheeks and pretended not to hear me as she sang. Her singing made me sad because I knew why she had cried, and she knew I knew. I seized the opportunity to

Dialogue

say, "I don't want an arranged marriage," but she sang on even louder, singing a song of a distant home. In times such as these, like my

Outcome

father, she too covers her ears with the thick dried mud of tradition. She doesn't want to

Meaning

hear me. It is easier that way.

Exercise 2   Discussion and Critical Thinking

1. Why did Shastri's mother cry?

2. What chance does Shastri have to make her own choice?

3. What would you advise her to do?

4. How does the specific example of Shastri's mother crying imply more than it actually says?

Professional Writing

*Dark Day in the Dust Bowl** [3rd-person POV]

John Steinbeck

> *In the 1930s, a dust storm descended on the Southwest. The sun disappeared, the chickens went to roost in the middle of the day, a desert invaded the fields, and sand drifted in like snow, in places covering whole houses. Initially, some people, especially those in rural areas, thinking the end of the world was upon them, fled to churches or withdrew into themselves. But then they found the strength to survive, some digging out and digging in, some moving out and moving away. In* The Grapes of Wrath, *from which this excerpt is taken, John Steinbeck depicts the people in an early stage of confronting this natural disaster.*

The people came out of their houses and smelled the hot stinging air and covered their nose from it. And the children came out of their houses, but they did not run or shout as they would have done after a rain. Men stood by their fences and looked at the ruined corn, drying fast now, only a little green showing through the film of dust. The men were silent and did not move often. And the women came out of the houses to stand beside their men—to feel whether this time the men would break. The women studied the men's faces secretly, for the corn could go, as long as something else remained. The children stood nearby, drawing figures in the dust with bare toes, and the children sent exploring senses out to see whether men and women would break. The children peeked at the faces of the men and women, and then drew careful lines in the dust with their toes. Horses came to the watering troughs and nuzzled the water to clear the surface dust. After a while the faces of the watching men lost their bemused perplexity and became hard and angry and resistant. Then the women knew that they were safe and that there was no break. Then they asked, What'll we do? And the men replied, I don't know. But it was all right. The women knew it was all right, and the watching children knew it was all right. Women and children knew deep in themselves that no misfortune was too great to bear if their men were whole. The women went into the houses to their work, and the children began to play, cautiously at first. As the day went

---

*Title by editor.

forward the sun became less red. It flared down on the dust-blanketed land. The men sat in the doorways of their houses; their hands were busy with sticks and little rocks. The men sat still—thinking—figuring.

From John Steinbeck, *The Grapes of Wrath*
(New York: Scribner's), p. 1.

Exercise 3   Discussion and Critical Thinking

1. Notice how each group looks at something. What do the men look at? What do the women look at? What do the children look at?

2. What is more important, finding a solution to the problem or finding courage to face the problem?

3. Explain how this incident could be a pivotal moment for any person here but especially for the children.

4. Briefly, what are the situation, the conflict, the struggle, the outcome, and the meaning?

   Situation: _____

   Conflict: _____

   Struggle: _____

   Outcome: _____

   Meaning: _____

5. How does descriptive detail heighten the tension? In other words, what is emphasized?

6. What words or phrases suggest the passage of time and give chronological order to this piece?

⌒ Topics for Paragraphs of Narration

Most of these topics can also be used for short essays.

Reading-Based Writing Topics

See Chapter 5 for instruction and examples for writing summaries, reactions, and two-part responses (separate paragraphs of summary and reaction). Use quotations and references. Credit source(s).

"Yearning for Love"

1. Assume that you are a psychologist or the personal-advice columnist for a large newspaper and Chantra Shastri has written her paragraph to you. Realizing that she has a life ahead of her and her family is asking her to choose between independence and family, what would you suggest that she do? Another possible aspect of the issue: Take into account that Shastri's parents might say to you that most American marriages end in divorce and that they, the parents, could make a better decision for a sound marriage, one that is less immature, less emotional, and less hormonal—one that is based on what they know about both their daughter and the young man they had already selected. Refer directly to the paragraph and use quotations.

"Dark Day in the Dust Bowl"

2. Write about how the idea of courage, or of attitude, can influence behavior. Refer to the children, the women, and the men. Use quotations and references.

3. Pretend that you were there as a child and write about what happens from your (first-person) point of view; that is, describe how you feel during the story as you react to how the women and men behave. Include the same details about the effects of the dust; if you use the same phrases that Steinbeck used, though, enclose those phrases in quotation marks. Be sure to do it as you report from the *I* perspective, such as "I could see that all the mothers were...." You can refer to what was happening to the children by saying, for example, we "acted," "watched," "saw," "felt," "started feeling different," and so on. Discuss the behavior of all three parts of the group: the (other) children, the women, and the men.

4. Write about a time when you or your family felt threatened and then drew strength from the courage of a family member or group leader. Explain how that was different from and similar to the narrative written by Steinbeck. Use quotations and references.

General Topics

5. Write a narrative paragraph about the first time you did something, such as the first time you dated, kissed romantically, spoke formally in public, entered a new school, worked for pay, drove an automobile, rode a bicycle or motorcycle, danced, received a traffic citation, met a celebrity, tried out for a sports team or a club or other "social" group, confessed you did something wrong, applied for a job, or met your date's parents.
6. Write a narrative paragraph about a personal experience that you might characterize as the most amusing, sad, terrifying, satisfying, stupid, rewarding, self-centered, generous, stingy, loving, thoughtful, cruel, regrettable, educational, corrupting, sinful, virtuous, or disgusting thing you have done or witnessed. Keep in mind that you are writing about a single event or a portion of that event. For a helpful model on a similar topic, review "Struggling Against Silence" on page 51.

Cross-Curricular Topics

7. Write a case study of an individual's behavior in a class requiring observation, such as teacher training, physical education, sociology, psychology, or business management.
8. Write a report on how you completed an experiment in a class (biology, ecology, psychology).
9. Describe a pivotal moment or revealing incident in the life of a historical figure, a composer, an artist, or an author.

Career-Related Topics

10. Write a narrative paragraph about learning how to do something specific on the job. In what way(s) did you or someone else perform badly, perhaps ridiculously? Many of these events occur on the first day of employment. For a helpful model on a similar topic, review "King of Klutziness" on page 70.

11. Write a narrative paragraph about a work-related encounter between a manager and a worker, and briefly explain the significance of the event.
12. Write a narrative paragraph about an encounter between a customer and a salesperson. Explain what went right and what went wrong.
13. Write a narrative paragraph about how a person solved a work-related problem.
14. Write a narrative paragraph about a salesperson's dealing with a customer's complaint. Critique the procedure.

Writer's Guidelines at a Glance: Narration

1. Use this checklist to be sure you have a complete narrative.

   - Situation (at beginning)
   - Conflict
   - Struggle
   - Outcome
   - Meaning

2. Use these devices as appropriate:

   - Images (sight, sound, smell, taste, touch) and other details to advance action
   - Dialogue
   - Transitional words (such as *after*, *finally*, *following*, *later*, *next*, *soon*, *when*) to enhance chronological order

3. Consider using the Brandon Writing Process Worksheet with the Brandon Guide for Revising and Editing (see the form that can be enlarged and copied from inside the front of this book). Then, after your assignment is returned, update the Self-Evaluation chart on the back of the front cover.

7

Description:
Moving Through
Space and Time

～ Writing Paragraphs of Description

Description is the use of words to represent the appearance or nature of something. Often called a **word picture**, description attempts to present its subject for the mind's eye. In doing so, it does not merely become an indifferent camera; instead, it selects details that will depict something well. Just what details the descriptive writer selects will depend on several factors, especially the type of description and the dominant impression in the passage.

Types of Description

On the basis of treatment of subject material, description is customarily divided into two types: objective and subjective.

Effective **objective description** presents the subject clearly and directly as it exists outside the realm of feelings. If you are explaining the function of the heart, the characteristics of a computer chip, or the renovation of a manufacturing facility, your description would probably feature specific, impersonal details. Most technical and scientific writing is objective in that sense. It is likely to be practical and utilitarian, making little use of speculation and poetic technique while focusing on details of sight.

Effective **subjective description** is also concerned with clarity and it may be direct, but it conveys a feeling about the subject and sets a mood while making a point. Because most expression involves personal views, even when it explains by analysis, subjective description (often called **emotional description**) has a broader range of uses than objective description.

78

Descriptive passages can be a combination of objective and sub-jective description; only the larger context of the passage will reveal the main intent. The following description of a baseball begins with objective treatment and then moves to subjective.

*On the Ball**

Roger Angell

[A baseball] weighs just over five ounces and measures between 2.86 and 2.94 inches in diameter. It is made of a composition-cork nucleus encased in two thin layers of rubber, one black and one red, surrounded by 121 yards of tightly wrapped blue-gray wool yarn, 45 yards of white wool yarn, 53 more yards of blue-gray wool yarn, 150 yards of fine cotton yarn, a coat of rubber cement, and a cowhide (formerly horsehide) exterior, which is held together with 216 slightly raised cotton stitches. Printed certifications, endorse-ments, and outdoor advertising spherically attest to its authenticity. . . . Pick it up and it instantly suggests its purpose; it is meant to be thrown a considerable distance—thrown hard and with pre-cision. Its feel and heft are the beginning of the sport's critical dimensions; if it were a fraction of an inch larger or smaller, a few centigrams heavier or lighter, the game of baseball would be utterly different. Hold a baseball in your hand. As it happens, this one is not brand-new. Here, just to one side of the curved surgical welt of stitches, there is a pale-green grass smudge, darkening on one edge almost to black—the mark of an old infield play, a tough grounder now lost in memory. Feel the ball, turn it over in your hand; hold it across the seam or the other way, with the seam just to the side of your middle finger. Speculation stirs. You want to get outdoors and throw this spare and sensual object to somebody or, at the very least, watch somebody else throw it. The game has begun.

Imagery

To convey your main concern effectively to readers, you will have to give some sensory impressions. These sensory impressions, col-lectively called **imagery**, refer to that which can be experienced by the senses—what we can see, smell, taste, hear, and touch.

Subjective description is more likely to use images and words rich in associations than is objective description. But just as a fine line cannot always be drawn between the objective and the subjective, a

*Paul Gallico, *The Golden People* (New York: Doubleday, 1965), p. 17.

fine line cannot always be drawn between word choice in one and in the other. However, we can say with certainty that whatever the type of description, careful word choice will always be important.

General and Specific Words

To move from the general to the specific is to move from the whole class or body to the individual(s); for example:

General	Specific	More Specific
food	pastry	Twinkie
mess	grease	oil slicks on table
drink	soda	mug of root beer
odor	smell from grill	smell of frying onions

Abstract and Concrete Words

Words are classified as abstract or concrete depending on what they refer to. **Abstract words** refer to qualities or ideas: *good, ordinary, ultimate, truth, beauty, maturity, love.* **Concrete words** refer to sub-stances or things; they have reality: *onions, grease, buns, tables, food.* The specific concrete words, sometimes called **concrete particulars**, often support generalizations effectively and convince the reader of the accuracy of the account.

Dominant Impression

Never try to give all of the details in description; instead, be selec-tive, picking only those that you need to make a dominant impres-sion, always taking into account the knowledge and attitudes of your readers. Remember, description is not photographic. If you wish to describe a person, select only those traits that will present the person according to your concerns. If you wish to describe a landscape, do not give all the details that you might find in a photo; just pick the details that support what you want to say. That extremely important dominant impression is directly linked to your purpose and is created by choosing and arranging images and other revealing details.

Order: Time and Space

All of the details must have some order. Time and space are the main controlling factors in most description.

If you were describing something that was not changing—a room, for example—you would be concerned with space and give directions to the reader such as *next to, below, under, above, behind, in front of, beyond, in the foreground, in the background, to the left,* or *to the right.*

If you were describing something that was changing, such as a butterfly going through metamorphosis, you would be concerned mainly with time and use transitional words such as *first, second, then, soon, finally, while, after, next, later, now,* or *before.*

If you were walking through an area—so that the setting was changing—you would use both time and space for order.

Transitional Words

Consider using the following transitional words to improve coherence by connecting ideas with ideas, sentences with sentences, and paragraphs with paragraphs:

- **FOR DESCRIPTION Place:** *above, over, under, below, nearby, near, across, beyond, among, to the right, to the left, in the background, in the foreground, further, beside, opposite, within sight, out of sight*

- **FOR NARRATION AS PART OF DESCRIPTION Time:** *after, before, later, earlier, initially, soon, recently, next, today, tomorrow, yesterday, now, then, until, currently, when, finally, not long after, immediately, (at) first, (at) last, third, previously, in the meantime, meanwhile*

Procedure at a Glance

What is your subject? (school campus just before the fall semester begins)

What is the dominant impression? (deserted)

What details support the dominant impression?

1. Smell of flowers and cut grass rather than food and perfume
2. Dust accumulated on white porcelain drinking fountain
3. Sound of the wind, wildlife, and silence rather than people
4. Crunch of dead leaves underfoot
5. Echo of footsteps

What is the situation? (You are walking across the campus in early August.)

What is the order of details? (time, place, or both)

⌒ Practicing Patterns of Description

Exercise 1 Completing Patterns

Fill in the blanks in the following outline to complete the description.

Shopping in a Supermarket Produce Area (Dominant impression: Diversity of products)

I. Food displays (sight—color, shape)

    A. _____

    B. _____

    C. _____

II. Smells (from vegetables, fruits)

    A. _____

    B. _____

III. Textures (smooth or rough to touch)

    A. _____

    B. _____

IV. Taste (samples of sweet/sour, ripe/unripe)

    A. _____

    B. _____

⌒ Examining Paragraphs of Description

Student Writing

My Burning Scarf

Julie Lee

Student Julie Lee writes about a scarf that was mistakenly burned in a family ceremony. Her attention to descriptive detail highlights this vivid recollection and conveys the poignancy of her experience. Be prepared to discuss this as narration.

Dominant impression   During my childhood, my <u>favorite</u> <u>possession</u> was the yellow scarf my dad

Topic sentence	gave me when I was five. <u>It would bring me pleasure and pain</u>. Hand-sewn with care in Japan, it attracted many curious and envious eyes. Needless to say, I was the proud owner of that scarf and loved the attention it
Objective descriptive details	brought me. The scarf was about <u>two feet square and made of pure virgin wool</u>. <u>It was decorated with a fringed green edge,</u>
Images: sight	<u>and in one corner five embroidered yellow-colored chicks played against the background needlework of lush green grass</u>. The material
Images: touch	was as <u>soft as cashmere</u> and had the <u>warmth of fur</u>. It kept my cheeks warm when I wrapped it loosely around my neck. But when I was six, I let my seriously ill sister wear my scarf to the doctor's office. She didn't give it back to me immediately, and because she was sick I didn't ask for it. Sadly, she died of leukemia after months of suffering. A few
Images: sight	days after she died, from my bedroom I <u>saw my mother</u> in the backyard <u>burning personal items</u> that belonged to my dead sister. It is a Korean custom to do so. My mother was crying and so were other adults standing in a circle around the fire. Then I saw my mother pick
Images: sight	up my <u>wadded yellow scarf</u> and shake it out. I rushed outside, shrieking for her to stop.
Images: sound	Over the sounds of <u>sobbing</u> and the <u>popping</u> of the fire, I wanted to shout, "That's my scarf, my precious possession." But I didn't, and my mother, thinking I was crying only for my sister, flung it into the flames of the
Images: sound	fire that <u>sizzled and cracked</u>, and the green and yellow of my childhood turned to orange, then red, then gray.

Professional Writing

*The Road to Cedar City**

William Least Heat-Moon

> *William Trogdon, of English-Irish-Osage ancestry, writes under the pen name William Least Heat-Moon. Traveling around the country in an old van he named Ghost Dancing, he sought out interesting locales on secondary highways marked in blue on road maps. His descriptive narratives of these adventures were published in the best-selling book* Blue Highways, *from which this paragraph is taken.*

At dusk I considered going to the Coral Sand Dunes for the night, but I'd had enough warmth and desert for a while, so I pushed north toward Cedar Breaks in the severe and beautiful Markagunt Plateau. The cool would refresh me. Sporadic splats of rain, not enough to pay attention to, hit the windshield. I turned onto Utah 14, the cross-mountain road to Cedar City. In the dim light of a mountainous sky, I could just make out a large sign.

> ELEVATION 10,000 FEET
> ROAD MAY BE IMPASSABLE
> DURING WINTER MONTHS.

So? It was nearly May. The rain popped, then stopped, popped and stopped. The incline became steeper and light rain fell steadily, rolling red desert dust off the roof; I hadn't hit showers since east Texas. It was good. The pleasant cool turned to cold, and I switched on the heater. The headlights glared off snowbanks edging closer to the highway as it climbed, and the rain became sleet. That's when I began thinking I might have made a little miscalculation. I looked for a place to turn around, but there was only narrow, twisted road. The sleet got heavier, and the headlights were cutting only thirty feet into it. Maybe I could drive above and out of the storm. At eight thousand feet, the wind came up—a rough, nasty wind that bullied me about the slick road. Lear,** daring the storm to "strike flat the thick rotundity of the world," cries, "Blow, winds! . . . Rage! Blow!" And that's just what they did.

*William Least-Heat Moon, *Blue Highways* (Boston: Little, Brown, and Company, 2012), p. 214.

**The main character in William Shakespeare's play *King Lear*.

Exercise 2 Discussion and Critical Thinking

1. What is the dominant impression of the descriptive paragraph by William Least Heat-Moon?

2. What support does he use for the dominant impression?

3. Give an example of each of these kinds of images:

   Sight:

   Sound:

   Touch:

4. Is the description organized by time or space or both? Explain.

∿ Topics for Paragraphs of Description

Most of these topics can also be used for short essays.

Reading-Based Writing Topic

See Chapter 5 for instruction and examples for writing summaries, reactions, and two-part responses (separate paragraphs of summary and reaction). Use quotations and references. Credit source(s).

"My Burning Scarf"

1. Write a reaction to this descriptive paragraph in which you explain how the meaning incorporates personal needs, family, and culture (perhaps using those headings for your outline). Explain how Lee's use of a narrative framework makes the passage more compelling. As an option, you could use the narrative framework (situation, conflict, struggle, outcome, and meaning) as main points in your outline for discussing this paragraph. Use references and quotations.

General Topics

Objective Description

2. Describe a ball (other than a baseball)—basketball, golf ball, tennis ball, soccer ball—or another piece of sports equipment that can be depicted objectively but often inspires a subjective reaction. It might be helpful to include a photo or a drawing of your subject. For a useful model on a similar subject, review "On the Ball" on page 79.

Subjective Description

3. Write a highly descriptive paragraph about a possession you received or purchased, treasured, and—somehow—lost, perhaps through theft, your carelessness, wear and tear, or someone else's neglect or spiteful act. Describe it well, but locate the possession within the framework of a little story. For a useful model on a similar subject, review "My Burning Scarf" on page 82.

4. Describe a dramatic part of a difficult adventure you have experienced. It might be a difficult trip you took (as a driver or as a passenger, perhaps with an impaired driver) under bad conditions, such as fog, snow, rain, windstorm, hail, heat, or traffic congestion. Or it could be a scary walk or run you took in the darkness, in a remote area, or in any area that made you fearful. Consider quoting from any warning someone gave you prior to the adventure or any sign you encountered along the way. For a useful model paragraph on a similar subject, review "The Road to Cedar City" on page 84.

5. Personalize a trip to a supermarket, a stadium, an airport, an unusual house, a mall, a beach, a court, a place of worship, a club, a business, a library, or a police station. Describe a simple conflict in one of those places, while emphasizing descriptive details.

6. Pick a high point in any event, and describe a few seconds of it. Think about how a scene can be captured by a video camera, and then give focus by applying the dominant-impression principle, using the images of sight, sound, taste, touch, and smell that are relevant. The event might be a ball game, a graduation ceremony, a wedding ceremony, a funeral, a dance, a concert, a family gathering, a class meeting, a rally, a riot, a robbery, a fight, a proposal, or a meal. Focus on a body of subject material that you can cover effectively in the paragraph you write.

Cross-Curricular Topic

7. Select one of the following subject areas, and then use description to write the report.
    a. Agriculture: field-trip report
    b. Art History: report on a museum or a particular work of art
    c. Education: school-visit report
    d. Ecology: field-trip report
    e. Geology: field-trip report
    f. Sociology: report on a field trip to an urban zone, a prison, or another institution

Career-Related Topics

8. Describe a well-furnished, well-functioning office or other work area. Be specific.
9. Describe a product, with special attention to the dominant trait that gives the product its reputation.
10. Describe a person properly groomed and attired for a particular job or interview. Give specific details about the person and the place or situation. If you like, objectively describe yourself (to the best of your ability) as that specific person.

Writer's Guidelines at a Glance: Description

1. In an **objective description**, use direct, practical language and usually appeal mainly to the sense of sight.
2. In a **subjective** or an **emotional description**, appeal to the reader's feelings, especially through the use of images of sight, sound, smell, taste, and touch.
3. Use specific and concrete words if appropriate.
4. Be sure that readers can answer the following questions:
    What is the subject of this description?
    What is the dominant impression?
    What details support the dominant impression?
    What is the situation?
    What is the order of details—time, space, or both?
5. Consider using the Brandon Writing Process Worksheet with the Brandon Guide for Revising and Editing (see the form that can be enlarged and copied from inside the front of this book). Then, after your assignment is returned, update the Self-Evaluation Chart on the back of the front cover.

8

Exemplification:
Writing with Examples

~ Writing Paragraphs of Exemplification

Exemplification means using examples to explain, to convince, or to amuse. Lending interest and information to writing, exemplification is one of the most common and effective ways of developing ideas. Examples may be developed in a sentence or more, or they may be only phrases or even single words, as in the following sentence: "Children like packaged breakfast foods, such as *Wheaties, Cheerios,* and *Rice Krispies.*"

Characteristics of Good Examples

As supporting information, the best examples are vivid, specific, and representative. These three qualities are closely linked and, collectively, they must support the topic sentence. The **vivid** example attracts attention. Then through a memorable presentation and the use of identifying names, the example becomes **specific** to the reader. A good example must also be **representative**; that is, it must be experienced as typical so that it can be the basis for a generalization.

Finally, and most important, the **connection** between the example and the topic sentence must be clear. A bizarre case of cheating may be fascinating in itself (vivid and specific), but to be effective in a paragraph on "the hard work of cheating," it must also support the topic sentence. The reader should say, in effect, "That's interesting, convincing, and memorable. Though it's unusual, I can see that it's typical of what goes on."

Techniques for Finding Examples

Writing a good paragraph of exemplification begins, as always, with prewriting. The techniques you use will depend on what you are

88

writing about. Assuming that you begin with a topic idea, one useful technique is listing. Base your list on what you have read, heard, and experienced. Here is a list on the broad topic "cheating at school":

> When I copied homework
> Looking at a friend's test answers
> A student with hand signals
> Jake and his electronic system
> Time for planned cheating
> Those who got caught
> A person who bought a research paper
> Jess, who copied from me
> The Internet "Cheaters" source
> The two students who exchanged identities
> More work than it's worth
> More stress than it's worth

Connecting Examples with Purpose

Here is the final paragraph in an essay on the topic "the hard work of cheating."

Topic sentence	Cheating students often put themselves under more stress than honest students.
Extended example	I remember someone in my junior composition class who needed a research paper, so he found a source and bought one for seventy-five dollars. The first trouble was that he had to submit the work in stages: the topic, the working bibliography, the note cards, the outline, the rough draft, and the final paper. Therefore, he went to the library and started working backward. Of course, he couldn't turn in only the bib cards actually used in the paper, and next he had to make out note cards for the material he "would be" documenting, and even make out more. After having all kinds of trouble, he realized that the bought paper was of "A" quality, whereas he had been a "C" student. He went back to his source and was told he should change the sentence structure

Concluding sentence

and so on to make the paper weaker. Finally he dropped the class after spending more time on his paper than I did on mine. <u>He also suffered more anxiety than the students who put in the most work on their papers.</u>

Transitional Words

Consider using the following transitional words to improve coherence by connecting ideas with ideas, sentences with sentences, and paragraphs with paragraphs:

- **FOR EXEMPLIFICATION:** *for example, as an example, another example, for instance, such as, including, specifically, especially, in particular, to illustrate, as an illustration, that is, i.e.* (meaning *that is*), *e.g.* (meaning *for example*)

∿ Practicing Patterns of Exemplification

Exercise 1   Completing Patterns

Fill in the blanks in the following outlines to add more examples that support the topic sentences.

1. Topic sentence: Just walking through my favorite mall [or shopping center] shows me that the world is smaller than it used to be.

    I. People of different cultures (with specific examples)

    II. Foods of different cultures (with specific examples)

    III. _____

    IV. _____

2. Topic sentence: Driving to work [or school] this month and observing the behavior of other drivers have convinced me that road rage has invaded my community.

    I. A man honking his horn impatiently at an elderly driver

    II. _____

    III. _____

〜 Examining Paragraphs of Exemplification

Student Writing

Sweet and Sour Workplace
Sarah Betrue

A full-time student and a full-time worker, Sarah Betrue has a very busy life, which would go more smoothly if she did not have so many irritations. We are likely to identify with her experiences and to admire her for beginning and ending her work day in tranquility.

Every morning as I enter my workplace, I admire the vibrant colors of both the tropical fish in the aquarium and the ancient silk Chinese robes hung from the wall. But as I take the dreaded step from the dining area to the kitchen, the

Topic sentence scenery drastically changes. Stressful and frustrating situations occur daily behind the scenes at the restaurant, making it almost impossible for me to maintain a positive

Example attitude. Consider yesterday as a typical shift. The first voices I hear are the owners complaining about how filthy the restaurant looks, although the night before the other employees and I worked with Ajax for three hours scrubbing shelves and floor sinks. As the day progresses, I try to squeeze in some extra cleaning between busy times, but I find myself doing all the extra work myself. The young girls I work with think having this job is just an extension of their social lives. During lunch hour, the dining area is packed, the line for takeout has reached a ridiculous length, and two

Example phone calls are on hold. That's when Morgan

Example

decides to call her boyfriend on her cell
phone. Naturally I become frustrated and
proceed to speak with her. She glares at me
with fire in her eyes and screams, "I've got
more important things to deal with at this
time!" Getting nowhere with politeness, I
grab the phone from her hand and turn it
off. No sooner has this crisis ended than
the house phone rings again. On the line is
a very unhappy woman. After listening to a
few colorfully disparaging descriptions of a
meal she ordered, I tell her I cannot give
refunds or food exchanges if her order is
not returned first. She threatens to report
our restaurant to newspapers and authorities,
and then she tells me to do something I am
physically incapable of doing and hangs up in
my ear. At the end of the day I am so angry
and frustrated with having to put up with
such occurrences that I want to grab hold of
one of the woks and whack someone upside the
head. But just as I reach for the handle,
I get a vision, an image of my paycheck,
and I begin to relax. I leave the restaurant
with no blood on my hands, wishing everyone
a wonderful evening.

**Concluding
sentence**

Exercise 2   Discussion and Critical Thinking

1. What evidence shows that Betrue is not essentially a negative thinker?

2. What kind of order does Betrue use for her three specific supporting examples?

3. If you were one of the owners of the restaurant, how would you react to Betrue's paragraph?

Professional Writing

*Colorado Springs—Every Which Way** [3rd-person POV]

Eric Schlosser

> *In his best-selling book* Fast Food Nation, *Eric Schlosser exposes an ignorant and a largely uncaring society dependent on fast food. At the end of unsavory supply lines are rudderless cities thickly populated by fast-food chains serving up unhealthful food. One such city is Colorado Springs.*

Colorado Springs now has the feel of a city whose identity is not yet fixed. Many longtime residents strongly oppose the extremism of the newcomers, sporting bumper stickers that say, "Don't Californicate Colorado." The city is now torn between opposing visions of what America should be. Colorado Springs has twenty-eight Charismatic Christian churches and almost twice as many pawnbrokers, a Lord's Vineyard Bookstore and a First Amendment Adult Bookstore, a Christian Medical and Dental Society and a Holey Rollers Tattoo Parlor. It has a Christian summer camp whose founder, David Noebel, outlined the dangers of rock 'n' roll in his pamphlet *Communism, Hypnotism, and the Beatles.* It has a gay entertainment complex called The Hide & Seek, where the Gay Rodeo Association meets. It has a public school principal who recently disciplined a group of sixth-grade girls for reading a book on witchcraft and allegedly casting spells. The loopiness once associated with Los Angeles has come full-blown to Colorado Springs—the strange, creative energy that crops up where the future's consciously being made, where people walk the fine line separating a visionary from a total nutcase. At the start of a new century, all sorts of things seem possible there. The cultural and the physical landscapes of Colorado Springs are up for grabs.

*Eric Schlosser, *Fast Food Nation* (Boston: Houghton Mifflin, 2011), p. 59.

Exercise 3 Discussion and Critical Thinking

1. Which sentence is the better topic sentence, the first or the third? Explain why.

2. Use a phrase to indicate each example that supports the idea in the third sentence in the paragraph. Notice that the examples appear in contrasting patterns.

3. Does Schlosser seem to favor one vision of what America should be over the other? Do you? Discuss.

4. How does the last sentence function as part of the paragraph structure?

5. Discuss a city or a part of any community you are familiar with that is torn between opposing views of what America should be. Give some examples of establishments with implied contrasting values.

⌒ Topics for Paragraphs of Exemplification

Most of these topics can also be used for short essays.

Reading-Based Writing Topic

See Chapter 5 for instruction and examples for writing summaries, reactions, and two-part responses (separate paragraphs of summary and reaction). Use quotations and references. Credit source(s).

"Sweet and Sour Workplace"

1. Write a reaction in which you evaluate Betrue's essay. Does the example seem realistic as the experience of a young woman working in an ordinary job? What do you discover about her by

reading her paragraph? If you were an employer, would you offer her a job based on what you read here? Refer directly to the paragraph and use quotations.

General Topics

2. Write a paragraph or an essay about a town that seems to project different sets of values as it exhibits contradictory features such as institutions, stores, products, services, residents, and individual behavior. Rows of strip malls in your own or nearby communities may be especially rich locations for examples. For a helpful model of form on a similar topic, review "Colorado Springs—Every Which Way" on page 93.

3. Use examples to write a statement on how you have experienced and dealt with irritations at school, at home, at work, in a neighborhood, in theaters during a movie, in restaurants, on airplanes, on subways, on trains, on streets, or on highways. For a useful model on a similar topic, review "Sweet and Sour Workplace" on page 91.

4. Make a judgmental statement about a social issue you believe in strongly and then use an example or examples to illustrate your point. Some possible topics include the following:

   a. The price of groceries is too high.
   b. Professional athletes are paid too much.
   c. A person buying a new car may get a lemon.
   d. Drivers sometimes openly ignore the laws on a selective basis.
   e. Politicians should be watched.

Cross-Curricular Topics

5. Use examples to develop a generalization you make about one of these groups:

   a. Civil rights leaders
   b. Healthful foods
   c. Worthwhile exercises
   d. Influential artists (musicians, painters, composers, writers)
   e. Good parents
   f. Good coaches

6. Reports: Choose a subject and then write about it as being typical of a much larger group; for example, you could discuss one work

of art as typical in a museum exhibit of pieces grouped as Early French Impressionism, or you could analyze a typical student in a class visit you made for a special education class.

Career-Related Topic

7. Use specific examples to support or argue against one of the following statements as applied to business or work:

   a. It's not what you know, it's who you know.
   b. Don't burn your bridges.
   c. Like Lego, business is a matter of connections.
   d. The customer is always right.
   e. If you take care of the pennies, the dollars will take care of themselves.
   f. A kind word turns away wrath.

Writer's Guidelines at a Glance: Exemplification

1. Use examples to explain, convince, or amuse.
2. Use examples that are vivid, specific, and representative.

   - Vivid examples attract attention.
   - Specific examples are identifiable.
   - Representative examples are typical and therefore the basis for generalizations.

3. Tie your examples clearly to your topic sentence.
4. Draw your examples from what you have read, heard, and experienced.
5. Brainstorm a list of possible examples before you write.
6. Consider using the Brandon Writing Process Worksheet with the Brandon Guide for Revising and Editing (see the form that can be enlarged and copied from inside the front of this book). Then, after your assignment is returned, update the Self-Evaluation Chart on the back of the front cover.

9

Analysis by Division: Examining the Parts

~ Writing Paragraphs of Analysis by Division

Being able to analyze is the key to learning, performing, and teaching. If you need to explain how something works or exists as a unit, you will write an analysis by division. You will break down a unit (your subject) into its parts and explain how each part functions in relation to the operation or existence of the whole. The most important word here is *unit*. You begin with something that can stand alone or can be regarded separately. Here are some examples of topics, or general subjects, as units that can be divided into traits, characteristics, or other parts in different contexts by applying a specific principle (your focus):

- **Personal:** a relationship, love, a parent, a neighbor, a friend (traits)
- **Cross-Curricular:** a musical composition, a prepared food, an organism, a government
- **Career-Related:** a job description, an employee evaluation, a product, a service, a company

Procedure

The following procedure will guide you in writing an analysis by division. Move from subject to principle, to division, to relationship:

1. Begin with something that is a unit.
2. State the principle by which the unit functions or exists (your focus).
3. Divide the unit into parts according to that principle.
4. Discuss each part in relation to the unit.

You might apply that procedure to evaluating a restaurant in the following way:

1. Unit   Restaurant review
2. Principle of function   Overall quality
3. Parts based on the principle Ambiance (atmosphere), food, service
4. Discussion   Each part in relation to the quality
                                 of a dining experience

Organization

In a paragraph or an essay of analysis by division, the main parts are likely to be the main points of your outline or main extensions of your cluster. If they are anything else, reconsider your organization.

A basic outline of analysis by division might look like this:

Thesis: In judging this restaurant, one should consider these aspects.

  I. Ambiance
 II. Food
III. Service

Sequence of Parts

The order in which you discuss the parts will vary according to the nature of the unit and the way in which you view it. Here are some possible sequences for organizing the parts of a unit.

- **Time:** The sequence of the parts in your paragraph can be based on time if you are dealing with something that functions on its own, such as a heart, with the parts presented in relation to stages of the function.
- **Space:** If your unit is a visual object, especially if, like a statue, it does nothing by itself, you may discuss the parts in relation to space.
- **Emphasis:** Because the most emphatic part of any piece of writing is the end (the second-most emphatic point is the beginning), consider placing the most significant part of the unit at the end.

Transitional Words

Consider using the following transitional words to improve coherence by connecting ideas with ideas, sentences with sentences, and paragraphs with paragraphs:

- **FOR ANALYSIS BY DIVISION: Time or numbering:** *first, second, third, another, last, finally, soon, later, currently, before, along with, another part (section, component)*

- **Space:** *above, below, to the left, to the right, near, beyond, under, next to, in the background, split, divide*

- **Emphasis:** *most important, equally important, central to the, to this end, as a result, taken collectively, with this purpose in mind, working with the, in fact, of course, above all, most of all, especially, primarily, without question*

～ Practicing Patterns of Analysis by Division

Exercise 1 Completing Patterns

Fill in the blanks in the following outlines to complete each analysis by division.

1. Unit: Federal government

   Principle: Division of power

   Parts based on the principle:

   I. Executive

   II. _____

   III. _____

2. Unit: Good boss

   Principle: Effectiveness in leading a workforce

Parts based on the principle:

I. Fair

II. _____

III. _____

IV. _____

～ Examining Paragraphs of Analysis by Division

Student Writing

More Than Ordinary

Nancy Samuels

Faced with writing on the topic of "an example of a hero, with a discussion of the hero's traits [analysis by division]," Nancy Samuels didn't have to go to the library. Right in her household she found her subject—her mother. She writes about an ordinary person who faced a difficult challenge and succeeded in a situation in which others gave up.

Topic sentence	My mother is the best example of a hero I can think of. No one will read about her
Unit: hero	in a book about heroes, but in her small circle of friends, no one doubts her heroism.
Principle: strength	Certainly my younger brother doesn't. He is the special beneficiary of the strength of her heroism. He was in an accident when he was five years old, and the doctor told us that he would never walk again. My mother listened respectfully, but she didn't believe
I. Part one: Optimism	him. She had optimism. She went to another doctor and then another. Finally she found one who prescribed exercises. She worked

II. Part two: Perseverance with my brother for three years. Day after dismal day, she showed <u>perseverance</u>. It wasn't just her working with him that helped my brother.

III. Part three: Courage It was her raw <u>courage</u> in the face of failure. My brother worked with her. They both had courage. We other family members didn't. To us my brother and mother were acting like a couple of blind fools. We thought my mother especially, the leader, was in prolonged denial. But in three years my brother was walking. He won't be an athlete; nevertheless, he gets around. We're proud of him, but we know—and he knows—that without Mother he would never have walked. Of course, she's not a miracle worker. Most of the time, doctors are right, and some injured people can never walk. But the ones like my brother, who somewhere have that hidden ability, need

Concluding sentence that special someone like my mother. She's more than ordinary. <u>She's a hero</u>.

Exercise 2 Discussion and Critical Thinking

1. What are the main traits of Samuels's heroic mother?

2. Is she a miracle worker? Why or why not?

3. Will her kind of strength always succeed? Explain.

4. Would she have been considered heroic if she had not succeeded in helping her son?

Benjamin Franklin: Renaissance Person [3rd-person POV]
Allison Udell

Student Allison Udell uses analysis by division for a framework and develops her topic further with examples.

Topic sentence | Anyone who doesn't know the definition of *Renaissance person* (also known as a *polymath* or a *Renaissance man*) would do well to study Benjamin Franklin. When he died at eighty-four, he was acknowledged for being outstanding in many ways. One side

I. Support | of Benjamin Franklin was his education. He went to a formal school for only two years. But he learned six languages, published his own newspaper, and was recognized internationally as a scholar. A second field

II. Support | was his accomplishments as an inventor and a scientist. Almost everyone has heard of his experimentation with electricity, and his invention of bifocals, the lightning rod, the Franklin stove, and the school chair. However, Franklin did not restrict himself to books and the laboratory, for in his third

III. Support | field, he distinguished himself as an urban planner. He set the standard in designing a hospital, a library, a postal system, a city police department, and a city fire department. Finally, in his fourth field,

IV. Support | that of diplomat, he signed the Declaration of Independence, arranged for financial and military support from France, and helped negotiate the Treaty of Paris, which ended

Concluding sentence | the War of Independence. Clearly Benjamin Franklin is one of our greatest Renaissance persons—a top person in numerous fields.

Exercise 3 Discussion and Critical Thinking

1. What is the unit being analyzed?

2. What is the principle by which that unit functions? Write the answer here, or circle the passage that states or suggests the principle.

3. What are the parts that make up the unit according to this principle? Underline them in the text, or write them here.

4. What is the order of the parts (time, space, emphasis, or a combination)?

Professional Writing

The Mousetrap [3rd-person POV]

Craig Finley

> *Freelance writer Craig Finley begins this paragraph with a stark description of a conventional mousetrap and then dispassionately explains how it functions by examining the parts that work together as a unit. In a clear and concise presentation, his paragraph begins as a description and becomes an analysis by division, while also functioning as process analysis.*

The mousetrap is a remarkably simple and efficient instrument. The platform is a rectangular piece of soft pine wood, two and a half inches wide, six inches long, and a quarter-inch thick. The plane surface of the piece of wood is evenly divided by a square strike bar, which is attached to the middle by three staples. The staples are evenly spaced, with one in the middle. Between the middle and end staples on each side is a strong metal spring coiled around the bar. Each spring is taut and kept that way by the use of a straight piece of metal thrust out from the coil and tucked up under the strike bar on one side and placed against the board on the other. Also attached to the center of the strike bar is a bait pad, a little rectangular piece of flat metal with a grooved edge extending up from one side to hold the trigger rod. At the open end of the board, from an eye-screw, dangles the trigger rod, a long piece of metal that can move freely in a half circle from a point behind the screw to the grooved bait pad. To set the trap, place the bait, traditionally cheese, on the bait pad, then cock the strike bar by pulling the free end over in a half circle to the other side and tucking it under the trigger rod. Then secure the strike bar by moving the trigger rod into the groove on the side of the bait pad. When the rodent nibbles on the cheese, it will move the bait pad, which will loosen the trigger rod and, in turn, release the strike arc to pin the rodent against the board.

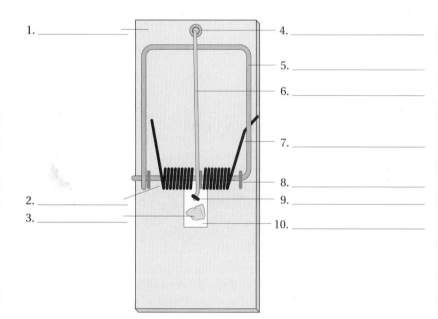

1. _____

2. _____

3. _____

4. _____

5. _____

6. _____

7. _____

8. _____

9. _____

10. _____

Exercise 4   Discussion and Critical Thinking

1. Underline the topic sentence.

2. Is the description objective or subjective?

3. Mark an X at the spot where the analysis by division moves from a description of parts and begins to explain how the parts function as an instrument.

4. Use phrases from the paragraph to label the ten parts of the drawing on page 104. If you are artistically inclined, add a rodent.

The Zones of the Sea [3rd-person POV]

Leonard Engel

> *In this paragraph reprinted from* The Sea, *published by Time-Life Books, the author shows that the sea can be divided into four zones.*

The life of the ocean is divided into distinct realms, each with its own group of creatures that feed upon each other and depend on each other in different ways. There is, first of all, the tidal zone, where land and sea meet. Then comes the realm of the shallow seas around the continents, which goes down to about 500 feet. It is in these two zones that the vast majority of marine life occurs. The deep ocean adds two regions, the zone of light and the zone of perpetual darkness. In the clear waters of the western Pacific, light could still be seen at a depth of 1,000 feet through the portholes of the *Trieste* on its seven-mile dive. But for practical purposes the zone of light ends at about 600 feet. Below that level there is too little light to support the growth of the "grass" of the sea—the tiny, single-celled green plants whose ability to form sugar and starch with the aid of sunlight makes them the base of the great food pyramid of the ocean.

Exercise 5 Discussion and Critical Thinking

1. What are the four zones of the sea?

2. Is the paragraph organized by space or by time?

3. What characterizes each zone?

4. Draw a cross section of the sea to show the four zones. Make it as elaborate with creatures and plants as you like. Consider using a separate sheet of paper for your drawing.

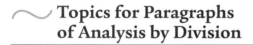

Topics for Paragraphs of Analysis by Division

Most of these topics can also be used for short essays.

Reading-Based Writing Topic

See Chapter 5 for instruction and examples for writing summaries, reactions, and two-part responses (separate paragraphs of summary and reaction). Use quotations and references. Credit source(s).

"More Than Ordinary"

1. Write a paragraph in which you disagree with Samuels's idea that an ordinary person can be a hero or because you believe that to regard an ordinary person as a hero is to cheapen the word. Give examples of one or more heroes whose behavior support your definition. Use references and quotations as you refer to the situation and the traits of the subject in this paragraph.

General Topics

2. Write about an ordinary person who has struggled mightily and deserves the title *hero*. Structure your piece around the person's achievements and traits, especially the traits. For a useful model, review "More Than Ordinary" on page 100.

3. In a paragraph of analysis by division, discuss the qualities that make someone or something successful or praiseworthy. Begin with a topic sentence such as this (modify it later to make it less mechanical): "[_____]'s success can be attributed to three [*or* four] qualities." The qualities would, of course, become the main parts of your outline. Select one of these subjects:

   a. A specific performer (a singer, a dancer, an actor, a musician)
   b. A team, a company, a school, a class, an organization
   c. A movie, a television program, a music video, a video game
   d. A family, a marriage, a relationship, a club

4. Discuss how a physical object works, perhaps a part of the body
   (the heart, the ear, the lungs), a part of a car (the carburetor, the
   water pump), or an object (a CD player, a stapler, a pencil sharp-
   ener, a hair dryer).

5. Write a restaurant review in which you discuss an eating place
   you are familiar with (a fast-food restaurant, the campus cafete-
   ria, an upscale restaurant). Use ambiance (atmosphere), service,
   and food as parts of your analysis by division. Name the place,
   narrate your visit, describe the particulars. See the first page of
   this chapter for guidance on this topic.

Cross-Curricular Topics

6. Consider the units of material in a class you are taking or have
   taken. Each unit has its parts: a musical composition in a music-
   appreciation class, a short story in an English class, an organ such
   as the heart in a biology class, a government in a political-science
   class, a management team in a business class, a family in a sociology class, a painting in an art-history class, a teacher or student
   in an education class, and so on. Select one unit, consult your
   textbook(s), talk to your instructor(s), and follow the procedure
   for writing an analysis by division. Credit your sources, and use
   quotation marks around material you borrow.

7. Select a unit from a class and discuss how it can be divided and
   the reasons for the division. It could be a heart, a brain, or skin
   in a life-science class or a tree trunk in a botany class. (For a
   good example of a similar topic, see "The Zones of the Sea" on
   page 105.) Then illustrate your analysis by division with your
   own labeled drawing of the unit.

Career-Related Topics

8. Write an analysis by division about a job description, a product,
   a company, or a service.

9. Explain how each of several qualities of a specific person—
   intelligence, sincerity, knowledgeability, communication skills,
   manner, attitude, appearance—makes that individual an effective salesperson, manager, or employee.

Writer's Guidelines at a Glance: Analysis by Division

1. Follow the procedure discussed in this chapter from (step 1) unit to (step 2) principle to (step 3) parts to (step 4) discussion.
2. Present the parts in a way that promotes order. Consider time, space, and emphasis.
3. Emphasize how the parts function in relation to the operation of the whole unit.
4. Your basic outline will probably look like this:

    I. Part 1
    II. Part 2
    III. Part 3

5. Consider using the Brandon Writing Process Worksheet with the Brandon Guide for Revising and Editing (see the form that can be enlarged and copied from inside the front of this book). Then, after your assignment is returned, update the Self-Evaluation Chart on the back of the front cover.

10

Process Analysis: Writing About Doing

~ Writing Paragraphs of Process Analysis

If you have any doubt about how frequently we use process analysis, just think about how many times you have heard people say, "How do you do it?" or "How is [was] it done?" Even when you are not hearing those questions, you are posing them yourself when you need to make something, cook a meal, assemble an item, take some medicine, repair your car, or figure out what happened. In your college classes, you may have to discover how osmosis occurs, how a rock changes form, how a mountain was formed, how a battle was won, or how a bill goes through the legislature.

If you need to explain how to do something or how something was (is) done, you will write a paper of **process analysis**. You will break down your topic into stages, explaining each so that your reader can duplicate or understand the process.

Two Types of Process Analysis: Directive and Informative

The questions "How do I do it?" and "How is [was] it done?" will lead you into two different types of process analysis—directive and informative.

Directive process analysis explains how to do something. As the name suggests, it gives directions and gives the reader instructions. It says, for example, "Read me, and you can bake a pie [tune up your car, solve a math problem, write an essay, take some medicine]." Because it is presented directly to the reader, it usually addresses the reader as "you," or it implies the "you" by saying something such as "First [you] purchase a large, fat wombat, and then [you]...." In the same way, this textbook addresses

109

you or implies "you" because it is a long how-to-do-it (directive process analysis) statement.

Informative process analysis explains how something was (is) done by giving data (information). Whereas the directive process analysis tells you what to do in the future, the informative process analysis tells you what has occurred or what is occurring. If it is something in nature, such as the formation of a mountain, you can read and understand the process by which it emerged. In this type of process analysis, you do not tell the reader what to do; therefore, you do not use the words *you* or *your*.

Working with Stages

Preparation

In the first stage of writing directive process analysis, list the materials or equipment needed for the process and discuss the necessary setup arrangements. For some topics, this stage will also provide technical terms and definitions. The degree to which this stage is detailed will depend on both the subject itself and the expected knowledge and experience of the projected audience.

Informative process analysis may begin with background or context rather than with preparation. For example, a statement explaining how mountains form might begin with a description of a flat portion of the earth made up of plates that are arranged like a jigsaw puzzle.

Steps

The actual process will be presented here. Each step must be explained clearly and directly, and it must be phrased to accommodate the audience. The language, especially in directive process analysis, is likely to be simple and concise; however, avoid dropping words such as *and, a, an, the,* and *of,* thereby lapsing into "recipe language." In directive process analysis the steps may be accompanied by explanations about why certain procedures are necessary and how not following directions carefully can lead to trouble. In informative process analysis the steps should appear in a logical progression within a sequence.

Order

The order will usually be chronological (time-based) in some sense.

Transitional Words

Consider using the following transitional words to improve coherence by connecting ideas with ideas, sentences with sentences, and paragraphs with paragraphs:

- **FOR PROCESS ANALYSIS:** *first, second, third, then, soon, now, next, finally, at last, therefore, consequently,* and— especially for informative process analysis—words used to show the passage of time, such as hours, days of the week, and so on.

Basic Forms

Consider using this form for directive process analysis (with topics such as how to cook something or how to fix something).

I. Preparation
   A.
   B.
   C.
II. Steps
   A.
   B.
   C.
   D.

Consider using this form for informative process analysis (with topics such as how a volcano functions or how a battle was won).

I. Background or context
   A.
   B.
   C.
II. Change or development (narrative)
   A.
   B.
   C.
   D.

～ **Practicing Patterns of Process Analysis**

Underlying a process analysis is a definite pattern. In some presentations, such as directions with merchandise to be assembled, the content reads as mechanically as an outline, and no reader objects. The same can be said of most recipes. In other presentations, such as your typical college assignments, the pattern is submerged in flowing discussion. The directions or information must be included, but the writing should be well developed and interesting. Regardless of the form you use or the audience you anticipate, keep in mind that in process analysis the pattern provides a foundation for the content.

Exercise 1   Completing Patterns

A. *Using directive process analysis, fill in the blanks in the following outline for replacing a flat tire with a spare. Work in a group if possible.*

   I. Preparation

      A. Park car.

      B. _____

      C. Obtain car jack.

      D. _____

      E. _____

  II. Steps

      A. Remove hub cap (if applicable).

      B. Loosen lug nuts a bit.

      C. _____

      D. _____

      E. Remove wheel with flat tire.

      F. _____

      G. _____

      H. Release jack pressure.

      I. _____

B. *Using informative process analysis, fill in the blanks in the following outline for an explanation of how a watermelon seed grows into a plant and produces a watermelon. Work in a group if possible.*

I. Background (what happens before the sprouting)

    A. Seed planted in cultivated land

    B. _____

    C. Receives heat (from sun)

II. Sequence (becomes plant and produces fruit)

    A. Sprouts

    B. _____

    C. Responds to sunlight and air

    D. _____

    E. _____

    F. Flower pollinated

    G. _____

∼ Examining Paragraphs of Process Analysis

Student Writing

Pupusas: Salvadoran Delight

Patty Serrano

We all have at least one kind of food that reminds us of childhood, something that has filled our bellies in times of hunger and perhaps comforted our minds in times of stress. For Patty Serrano, a community college student living at home, that special dish is pupusas. In El Salvador these are a favorite item in homes and restaurants and at roadside stands. In Southern California, they are available in little restaurants called pupusarias.

Every time my mom decides to make

Topic sentence pupusas, we jump for joy. <u>A pupusa contains only a few ingredients, and it may sound easy</u>

to make, but really good ones must be made
by experienced hands. My mom is an expert,
having learned as a child from her mother in

Preparation   El Salvador. All the ingredients are chosen
fresh. The meat, either pork or beef, can
be bought prepared, but my mom chooses to

Step 1   prepare it herself. The meat is ground and
cooked with tomatoes and spices. The cheese—
she uses a white Jalisco—has to be stringy
because that kind gives pupusas a very good
taste, appearance, and texture. Then comes

Step 2   the preparation of the "masa," or cornmeal.
It has to be soft but not so soft that it
falls apart in the making and handling.
All of this is done while the "comal," or
skillet, is being heated. She then grabs a

Step 3   chunk of masa and forms it into a tortilla
like a magician turning a ball into a thin

Step 4   pancake. Next she grabs small chunks of meat

Step 5   and cheese and places them in the middle of
the tortilla. The tortilla is folded in half

Step 6   and formed again. After placing the pupusa
into the sizzling skillet with one hand, she
is already starting another pupusa. It is
amazing how she does two things at the same

Step 7   time. She turns the pupusas over and over
again until she is sure that they are done.
We watch, mouths open, plates empty. In my
family it is a tradition that I get the first
pupusa because I like them so much. I love
opening the hot pupusas, smelling the aroma,
and seeing the stringy cheese stretching in
the middle. I am as discriminating as a wine
taster. But I never eat a pupusa without
"curtido," chopped cabbage with jalapeño.
Those items balance the richness of the

Concluding   other ingredients. <u>I could eat Mom's pupusas</u>
sentences   <u>forever</u>. <u>I guess it has something to do</u>
                   <u>with the way she makes them, with magical,</u>
                   <u>experienced, loving hands</u>.

Exercise 2   Discussion and Critical Thinking

1. Is this writing mainly informative or directive—or is it actually both? Explain.

2. Is Serrano's intended audience those who want to learn how to make *pupusas*, those who want to read about Serrano's love of *pupusas* as *pupusas* are related to her mother, or both?

3. What concrete details give this process analysis the feel of reality, meaning that Serrano knows what she is writing about?

Survival in the World of Zombies
Jerzy Kovac

Jerzy Kovac chose this from several prompts: "The setting should be a contemporary action movie; however, for this assignment, the movie is to be regarded as real life, and you will explain what the 'good-person' characters will have to know and do in order to survive." For a special exercise, he also wrote an essay on the same topic.

Wake up! While you were asleep last night, some strange illness started to affect the population of your town, at least it appears to be an illness. As you rub the sleepy sand from your eyes and lurch toward your kitchen window to get a good look at the new day, the world seems to be a little

different—a little off. One thing is for sure.
Your neighbor, Mr. Johanson, is not acting as he
usually does. Instead of saying his usual crisp
"Good Morning," as he walks his dog, Bridget, he
moans like a homesick Labrador, "Ahoooooo!" and
staggers up and down your street in pajamas with
his face smeared with ketchup—or is it blood?
Either way, things are getting pretty weird, and
they are getting weirder. When you turn on the news
footage of mobs of disheveled and vacant-eyed
people wandering aimlessly through your town
streets rolls for minutes on end. Ok, think hard,
and make yourself some coffee so that you can think
better. What do you believe is happening? That's
right, my friend. It's the end of the world, at
least the end of the world you are used to living
in. You now are a human in a world of zombies. And,
of course, zombies are human beings whose brains
have been infected with some noxious virus that
kills them but then allows them to come back as
mindless eating machines whose favorite food is
you—your brain, especially. Now you have to take
steps if you want to survive. Round up food, guns,
ammo, and try to get to a place without zombies.
Mr. Johanson is definitely a zombie, so your
neighborhood is no good. Better get in your car and
start driving. Forget about traffic laws; there are
no laws anymore. Get to the country away from those
darn creatures. If you get bitten, you will be
infected, too, and then you will become one of
them. Maybe you'll enter a real-life flash-mob
marathon, or maybe you'll crash an actual zombie
party.

Exercise 3 Discussion and Critical Thinking

1. The topic sentence is implied. Write a topic sentence that would fit.

2. What is the situation?

3. In the left margin, number the steps toward surviving.

4. In addition to process analysis, what other patterns of writing does Kovac use?

5. What must one know in order to survive?

6. What must one do?

Professional Writing

*Nature on the Rampage**

Ann Sutton and Myron Sutton

> *If you are about to die under tons of snow, ice, and debris and you have, say, one chance in thousands to live, what do you do? The Suttons offer steps that will at least increase your odds for survival.*

If you're caught, get moving! Ski or snowshoe as fast as you possibly can to the edge of the avalanche. Get rid of all of your accessories, or as many as you can, and do it at once—ski poles, pack, snowshoes, whatever you have. When the avalanche overtakes you, swim! This sounds ridiculous, but it's the best thing you can do to avoid being sucked under. Swim for your life, lying on your back if possible and with your feet downhill. Of course,

*From *Nature on the Rampage* by Ann Sutton and Myron Sutton (New York: Lippincott, 1962), p. 168.

you may have no choice, and the avalanche may tumble you whither it wishes, but do what you can to stay on the surface. Cover your mouth and nose—suffocation is easy in dry-snow avalanches. If you do get pulled under, make a supreme effort to widen a little airspace around you just as you come to a stop, and do it instantly! The snow may harden, pack and freeze almost at once. Then pray for help, and remember that the great Houdini made a living proving how long man could survive in tight and nearly airless spaces if he remained calm and confident and didn't panic. How to avoid panic in an avalanche is your problem.

Exercise 4   Discussion and Critical Thinking

1. What type of process analysis (informative or directive) is used?

2. To what type of audience (well informed, moderately informed, or poorly informed on the topic) does the writer direct this selection?

3. What is the prevailing tone (objective, humorous, reverent, argumentative, cautionary, playful, ironic, ridiculing) of this selection?

4. At which point do the preparation (materials, setup, explaining words, and so on) end and the steps begin? Underline the first sentence where the steps begin.

5. Write numbers in the margin to indicate the six steps, or stages, in the process.

∼ Topics for Paragraphs of Process Analysis

Most of these topics can also be used for short essays.

Reading-Based Writing Topic

See Chapter 5 for instruction and examples for writing summaries, reactions, and two-part responses (separate paragraphs of summary and reaction). Use quotations and references. Credit source(s).

"Survival in the World of Zombies"

1. In a reaction, explain the degree to which Jerzy Kovac's essay would be useful to a person who wishes to survive in a "World of Zombies." Evaluate its effectiveness for directions, word choice, and reasoning on a scale of one to five, with five being the highest. Be specific. Refer directly to the paragraph and use quotations.

General Topics

2. Using the topic quoted in the introduction to "Survival in the World of Zombies" on page 115 or in a frantic setting from one of your favorite action movies, explain the steps that would be necessary for you and others to survive.
3. Write about how your favorite meal is prepared by someone you know. Personalize this by putting it in the context of a household, perhaps even a special occasion such as a holiday or an ethnic celebration. For a model paragraph on a similar topic, review "Pupusas: Salvadoran Delight" on page 113.
4. Explain how to increase your chances for survival in a tornado, a hurricane, an earthquake, a fire in a high-rise building, or a flood. For a helpful model of form on a similar topic, review "Nature on the Rampage" on page 117.
5. Most of the topics in the following list are directive as they are phrased. However, each can be transformed into a how-it-was-done informative topic by personalizing it and explaining stage by stage how you, someone else, or a group did something. For example, you could write either a directive process analysis about how to deal with an obnoxious person or an informative process analysis about how you or someone else dealt with an obnoxious person. Keep in mind that the two types of process analysis, informative and directive, are often blended, especially in the personal approach. Many of the following topics will be more interesting to you and your readers if they are personalized, and most of them will require some narrowing to be treated in a paragraph. For example, writing about playing baseball is too broad; writing about how to

throw a curve ball may be manageable. Select a topic from the following list and write a paragraph

a. How to pass a test for a driver's license
b. How to get a job at [   ] _____
c. How to eat or prepare [   ] _____
d. How to teach a dog to behave or perform a trick
e. How to repair or assemble [   ] _____
f. How to end a relationship without hurting someone's feelings

Cross-Curricular Topics

6. Write a paragraph about a procedure you follow in your college work in a science (chemistry, biology, geology) lab. You may explain how to analyze a rock, how to dissect something, how to operate something, or how to perform an experiment.
7. Write a paragraph about how to do something in an activity or a performance class, such as drama, physical education, art, or music.

Career-Related Topics

8. Explain how to display, package, sell, or demonstrate a product.
9. Explain how to perform a service or how to repair or install a product.
10. Explain the procedure for operating a machine, a computer, a piece of equipment, or another device.

Writer's Guidelines at a Glance: Process Analysis

1. Decide whether your process analysis is mainly directive or mainly informative, and be appropriately consistent in using pronouns and other designations.

   ▪ For the directive process analysis, use the second person, addressing the reader as *you*. The *you* may be understood, even if it is not written.
   ▪ For the informative process analysis, use the first person or the third person:

a. Use the first person, speaking as *I* or *we*.

b. Use the third person, speaking about the subject as *he, she, it,* or *they,* or by name.

2. Consider using these basic forms:

Directive	Informative
I. Preparation	I. Background or context
A.	A.
B.	B.
II. Steps	II. Change or development
A.	A.
B.	B.
C.	C.

3. In explaining the stages and using technical terms, take into account whether your audience will be mainly well informed, moderately informed, or poorly informed.

4. Use transitional words indicating time or other progression (such as *first, second, then, soon, now, next, after, before, when, finally, at last, therefore, consequently,* and—especially for informative process analysis—words that show the passage of time, such as hours, days of the week, and so on).

5. Avoid using recipe language by not dropping *the, a, an,* or *of.*

6. Consider using the Brandon Writing Process Worksheet with the Brandon Guide for Revising and Editing (see the form that can be enlarged and copied from inside the front of this book). Then, after your assignment is returned, update the Self-Evaluation Chart on the back of the front cover.

11

Cause and Effect: Determining Reasons and Outcomes

~ Writing Paragraphs of Cause and Effect

Cause-and-effect relationships are common in our daily lives. A single situation may raise questions about both causes and effects:

> *The car won't start.*
> *Why?* (cause)
> *What now?* (effect)

In a paragraph, you will probably concentrate on either causes or effects, although you may mention both of them. Because you cannot write about all causes or all effects, you should try to identify and develop the most important ones. Consider that some causes are immediate, others remote; some visible, others hidden. Any one or a group of causes can be the most important. The effects of an event can also be complicated. Some may be immediate, others long range. The sequence of events is not necessarily related to causation. For example, *B* (inflation) may follow *A* (the election of a president), but that sequence does not mean that *A* caused *B*.

Researching and Organizing Cause and Effect

One useful approach to developing a cause-and-effect analysis is **listing**. In the middle of the page write down the event, situation, or trend that is your subject. Then, on the left side of the page list the causes and on the right side list the effects. Looking at the two lists, determine the better side (causes or effects) for your study.

122

Causes	Event, Situation, or Trend	Effects
Bad habits		Financial problems
In-law problems		Liberation
Religious differences		Financial success
Career decision		Safety
Personal abuse	*Divorce*	New relationships
Infidelity		Social adjustment
Sexual incompatibility		Vocational choice
Politics		Problems for children
Money		Independence

First, evaluate the items on your list. Keep in mind that one cause, such as personal abuse, may have its own (remote, hidden, or underlying) cause or partial cause: frustration over job loss, mental-health problems, drug addiction, bad parenting, or weak character. In single paragraphs, one usually deals with immediate causes, such as in-law problems, money, and personal abuse. (These same principles can be applied to effects.)

After you have evaluated the items on your list, choose two or three of the most important causes or effects and proceed. Be sure they relate directly to your topic sentence, or controlling purpose.

The causes could be incorporated into a preliminary topic sentence and then developed in an outline.

> *Preliminary topic sentence:* The main causes of my divorce were in-law problems, money, and personal abuse.

I. In-law problems
  A. Helped too much
  B. Expected too much
II. Money
  A. Poor management
  B. Low-paying job
III. Personal abuse
  A. Verbal
  B. Physical

On page 125, you can read the final, complete paragraph, "A Divorce with Reasons," by student Sarah Bailey, based on this outline.

Your paragraph will derive its structure from either causes or effects, although both causes and effects may be mentioned. Give emphasis and continuity to your writing by repeating key words, such as *cause, reason, effect, result, consequence,* and *outcome.*

The basic structure of your paragraph may look like this:

> Topic sentence
> Cause (or Effect) 1
> Cause (or Effect) 2
> Cause (or Effect) 3

Order

The order of the causes and effects you discuss in your paragraph may be based on time, space, emphasis, or a combination. Using transitional words will help in indicating that order.

Transitional Words

Consider using the following transitional words to improve coherence by connecting ideas with ideas, sentences with sentences, and paragraphs with paragraphs:

- **FOR CAUSE AND EFFECT: Cause:** *as, because, because of, due to, for, for the reason that, since, bring about, another cause, for this reason, one cause, a second cause, another cause, a final cause*
- **Effect:** *accordingly, finally, consequently, hence, so, therefore, thus, as a consequence, as a result, resulting*

〜 Practicing Patterns of Cause and Effect

Exercise 1   Completing Patterns

Fill in the blanks to complete first the causes outline and then the effects outline.

1. Causes for immigrating to the United States

    I. Desire for a better education

    II. _____

III. _____

IV. _____

2. Effects of getting adequate exercise

I. Muscle tone

II. _____

III. _____

IV. _____

⁓ Examining Paragraphs of Cause and Effect

Student Writing

A Divorce with Reasons

Sarah Bailey

A few years have passed, and student Sarah Bailey can look back on her divorce and sort out the causes and effects of her failed marriage. This paragraph, which focuses on three main causes, was developed through the listing and outlining shown on page 000.

I. Cause 1: In-law problems

I was married for almost five years. The first year was great, but each of the last four was worse than the previous one. The marriage was made in carefree leisure, and the divorce was made in a reality that just got colder and colder. Our first problem was the in-laws, actually his parents; mine live in another state, and we saw them only once a year. It was nothing deliberate. His parents wanted to help, and that was the problem. They expected me to be the daughter they never had and him to be a successful businessman and homeowner. They expected

**II. Cause 2:
Money**

too much from both of us, and we couldn't
make our own choices. <u>That cause was related
to another one—money</u>. Both of us had low-
level jobs in industry. We were around
people who were wealthy, but we couldn't
buy, belong, and participate as we wanted
to. Then I started getting more promotions
than he. Finally, he quit his job just at the
beginning of a recession, and he couldn't get
another one. I told him I would be patient,
but at times I was resentful that I was the
only one working. As he became more and more
frustrated, he started losing his temper with

**III. Cause
3: Abuse
A. Personal
B. Physical**

me and said things that <u>hurt my feelings</u>. <u>One
day he hit me</u>. He said he was sorry and even
cried, but I could not forgive him. We got a
divorce. It took me a while before I could
look back and see what the causes really
were, but by then it was too late to make any
changes.

Exercise 2   Discussion and Critical Thinking

1. Bailey says it took her too long to discover the causes of her divorce, so she was unable to deal with the problems. Looking at this case in speculation, would you say the problems can be found mainly in character or circumstance? Explain.

2. If Bailey had chosen to include more discussion of the effects of this divorce, what might she have mentioned?

More Than the Classroom
Richard Blaylock

Responding to an assignment on a topic organized mainly around causes and effects, Richard Blaylock chose to write about the consequences of his becoming a college student. With much trepidation, at thirty-three he had enrolled in the evening program at a local community college. The reasons for his being there were multiple, and so, surprising to him, were the results.

"We think you would benefit from our work-study program," he said to me. He wasn't my high school counselor, and I wasn't eighteen. He was the division manager, and he had just offered to pay my expenses for attending a local community college. At thirty-three, I was working for a large company in a dead-end job, dead-end because I wasn't qualified for any management positions. Naturally, I enrolled in college. More benefits than I expected were to follow. I had hardly started when the first response greeted me: my family was clearly proud. I heard my two kids in elementary school bragging about me to kids in the neighborhood. They even brought me some of their tough homework questions. My wife had lots of questions about college. We talked about taking a class together. Unlike me, she had been a good student in high school. Then I had had no interest in going on to college. Now I did, and one thing led to another. A geography class connected me with a geology class. A political-science class moved me to subscribe to the *Los Angeles Times*. I became more curious about a variety of subjects, and I felt more confident in dealing with ideas. At work my supervisors started asking me to become more involved in ongoing projects and planning. By the time I had taken my second English class, I was writing reports with much more confidence and skill. Now, after receiving a good job review and being interviewed by

```
my plant manager, I am in line for a promotion that
I once thought was beyond my reach. I had expected
a classroom. I found much more.
```

Exercise 3   Discussion and Critical Thinking

1. What is the subject and what is the focus of this paragraph?

2. Is this a paragraph mainly of causes or of effects? Explain.

3. List each effect—the benefits.

4. Show how narration is used as the framework for this cause-and-effect paragraph.

   Situation:

   Conflict:

   Struggle:

   Outcome:

   Meaning:

Professional Writing

Consumer Culture Rocks 'n' Rolls on the Scene*† [3rd-person POV]

David M. Kennedy and Lizabeth Cohen

David M. Kennedy and Lizabeth Cohen are both distinguished professors of history, Kennedy at Stanford University and Cohen at Harvard University. This excerpt is taken from the

*From *The American Pageant: A History of the American People,* 15th ed., by David M. Kennedy and Lizabeth Cohen (Boston: Wadsworth, 2013), pp. 863–64.

†Title by the author of this book.

fifteenth edition of The American Pageant: A History of the American People.

The 1950s witnessed a huge expansion of the middle class and the blossoming of a consumer culture. Popular music was dramatically transformed. The chief revolutionary was Elvis Presley, a white singer born in 1935 in Tupelo, Mississippi. Fusing black rhythm and blues with white bluegrass and country style, Elvis created a new musical idiom known forever after as rock 'n' roll. Rock was "crossover" music, carrying its heavy beat and driving rhythms across the cultural divide that separated black and white musical traditions. Listening and dancing to rock 'n' roll became a rite of passage for millions of young people around the world, from Japan to working-class Liverpool, England, where Elvis's music inspired teenagers John Lennon and Paul McCartney to form a band that would become the Beatles. Traditionalists were repelled by Presley, and they found much more to upset them in the affluent fifties. Movie star Marilyn Monroe, with her ingenuous smile and mandolin-curved hips, helped to popularize—and commercialize— new standards of sensuous sexuality. So did *Playboy* magazine, whose first issue Monroe graced in 1953. As the decade closed, Americans were well on their way to becoming free-spending consumers of mass-produced, standardized products, which were advertised on the electronic medium of television and often sold for their alleged sexual allure.

Exercise 4 Discussion and Critical Thinking

1. What two major changes took place during the cultural shift of the 1960s?

2. Who were the leaders of the two major forces?

3. Specifically, what changes occurred?

4. As further support for the topic sentence, what else is linked to Elvis and Marilyn?

5. If Elvis and Marilyn or others of similar influence had not existed, what do you think America would be like today?

6. What other entertainers or celebrities from recent history can challenge either Elvis or Marilyn as major causes of change in music or as sex symbols in society? Name and discuss them.

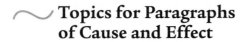

Topics for Paragraphs of Cause and Effect

Most of these topics can also be used for short essays.

Reading-Based Writing Topic

See Chapter 5 for instruction and examples for writing summaries, reactions, and two-part responses (separate paragraphs of summary and reaction). Use quotations and references. Credit source(s).

"Consumer Culture Rocks 'n' Rolls on the Scene"

1. Write a summary of this paragraph.
2. Write a two-part response to this paragraph.
3. Write a reaction to the paragraph. Refer to it directly and use quotations from it. Explain how other music styles have impacted cultural behaviour. For example, consider how hip-hop music has impacted culture in this contemporary generation: language, behavior, attitudes, dress styles, and so on.

General Topics

4. Write a paragraph about the causes or effects of a divorce on someone you know, either a divorced person or a relative of a divorced person. For a useful model on a similar topic, review "A Divorce with Reasons" on page 125.
5. Write about the causes for or effects of the good marriage of a couple you know.

6. Using "More Than the Classroom" on page 127 as a model, write a paragraph about the causes and the actual or anticipated effects of your going to college.
7. Write a paragraph about the causes of crime (for one individual involved in crime), unemployment (for one person who is out of work), leaving home (for one person who has left home), emigrating (for one person or family), poverty (for one person who is poor), school dropout (for one person), going to college (for one who did), or the success of a particular product or program on television.
8. Write a paragraph about the effects of disease (a particular disease, perhaps on just one person), fighting (one or two people involved in a dispute), fire (a particular one), alcoholism (a certain alcoholic), getting a job (a person with a particular job), early marriage (a person who married very young), teenage parenthood (one person or a couple), or dressing a certain way (one person and his or her style).

Cross-Curricular Topic

9. From a class that you are taking or have taken, select a subject that is especially concerned with causes and effects and develop a topic. Begin by selecting an event, a situation, or a trend in the class content and make a list of the causes or effects; that procedure will almost immediately show you whether you have a topic you can discuss effectively. Class notes and textbooks can provide you with more specific information. If you use textbooks or other materials, give credit to the sources. Instructors across the campus may have suggestions for studies of cause and effect. Some areas for your search include history, political science, geology, astronomy, psychology, philosophy, sociology, real estate, child development, education, fashion merchandising, psychiatric technician program, nursing, police science, fire science, physical education, and restaurant and food-service management.

Career-Related Topics

10. Discuss the effects (benefits) of a particular product or service on the business community, family life, society generally, specific groups (age, income, activities), or an individual.

11. Discuss the needs (thus the cause of development) by individuals, families, or institutions for a particular product or type of product.
12. Discuss the effects of using a certain approach, system, or philosophy in sales, human resources, or customer service.

Writer's Guidelines at a Glance: Cause and Effect

1. Have your purpose clearly in mind and find examples relating to that purpose.
2. Distinguish clearly between causes and effects by using three columns. From your lists, select only the most relevant causes or effects.

Causes	Event, Situation, or Trend	Effects

3. Concentrate primarily on either causes or effects. You may refer to both causes and effects, but use only one as the framework for writing your paragraph.
4. Do not conclude that something is an effect merely because it follows something else.
5. Emphasize your main concern, cause or effect, by repeating key words such as *cause, reason, effect, result, consequence,* and *outcome.*
6. Consider using the Brandon Writing Process Worksheet with the Brandon Guide for Revising and Editing (see the form that can

be enlarged and copied from inside the front of this book). Then, after your assignment is returned, update the Self-Evaluation Chart on the back of the front cover.

12

Classification:
Establishing Groups

∼ Writing Paragraphs of Classification

To explain by classification, you put persons, places, things, or ideas into groups, or classes, based on their characteristics. Whereas analysis by division deals with the parts of just one unit, classification deals with more than one unit, so the subject is plural.

To classify efficiently, try following this procedure:

1. Select a plural subject.
2. Decide on a principle for grouping the units of your subject.
3. Establish the groups, or classes.
4. Write about the classes.

Selecting a Subject

When you say you have different kinds of neighbors, friends, teachers, bosses, or interests, you are classifying; that is, you are forming groups.

In naming the different kinds of people in your neighborhood, you might think of different groupings of your neighbors, the units. For example, some neighbors are friendly, some are meddlesome, and some are private. Some neighbors have yards like Japanese gardens, some have yards like neat-but-cozy parks, and some have yards like abandoned lots. Some neighbors are affluent, some are comfortable, and some are struggling. Each of these sets is a classification system and could be the focus of one paragraph in your essay.

Using a Principle to Avoid Overlapping

All the sets in the preceding section are sound because each group is based on a single concern: neighborly involvement, appearance of

134

the yard, or wealth. This one concern, or controlling idea, is called the **principle**. For example, the principle of neighborly involvement controls the grouping of neighbors into three classes: friendly, meddlesome, and private.

All the classes in any one group must adhere to the controlling principle for that group. You would not say, for example, that your neighbors can be classified as friendly, meddlesome, private, and affluent, because the first three classes relate to neighborly involvement, but the fourth, relating to wealth, refers to another principle. Any one of the first three—friendly, meddlesome, and private—might also be affluent. The classes should not overlap in this way. Also, every member should fit into one of the available classes.

Establishing Classes

As you name your classes, rule out easy, unimaginative types such as *fast/medium/slow, good/average/bad*, and *beautiful/ordinary/ugly*. Look for creative, original phrases and unusual perspectives as shown in these simple forms.

Subject	Principle	Classes
neighbors	neighborhood involvement	friendly meddlesome private
neighbors	yard upkeep	immaculate neat messy
neighbors	wealth	affluent comfortable struggling

Complex classifications are based on one principle and then subgrouped by another related principle. The following example classifies neighbors by their neighborly involvement. It then subgroups the classes on the basis of motive.

I. Friendly

   A. Civic-minded

   B. Want to be accepted

   C. Gregarious

II. Meddlesome
    A. Controlling
    B. Emotionally needy
    C. Suspicious of others
III. Private
    A. Shy
    B. Snobbish
    C. Secretive

Transitional Words

Consider using the following transitional words to improve coherence by connecting ideas with ideas, sentences with sentences, and paragraphs with paragraphs.

- **FOR CLASSIFICATION:** *classify, (to) group, categorize, the first class, the second class, the third class, another class, a subclass, another subclass*

Exercise 1   Avoiding Overlapped Classes

Mark each set of classes as OK or OL (overlapping); circle the classes that overlap.

	Subject	Principle	Classes
EXAMPLE:	community college students	intentions	vocational academic transfer specialty needs (hardworking)
_____	1. airline flights	passenger seating	first class comfortable business coach

	Subject	Principle	Classes
_____	2. country singers	clothing trademark	hat overalls decorative costume expensive
_____	3. schools	ownership	private religious public
_____	4. faces	shape	round square oval beautiful broad long
_____	5. dates	behavior resembling aquatic animals	sharks clams jellyfish cute octopuses

∽ Practicing Patterns of Classification

Because the basic pattern of classification consists of classes, the initial outline is predictable: It uses Roman-numeral headings for the classes, although some classes may be longer and more complex than others.

Exercise 2   Completing Patterns of Classification

Fill in the blanks to identify classes that could be discussed for each subject.

1. *Subject:* Professional athletes

   Principle: Why they participate in sports

Classes:

   I. Glory

   II. _____

   III. _____

2. *Subject:* Pet owners

   Principle: Why they own [need] pets

   Classes:

      I. Companionship

      II. _____

      III. _____

3. *Subject:* Dates or prospective spouses

   Principle: The way they can be compared to vehicles

   Classes:

      I. Economy (Taurus, Corolla, Civic)

         A. Low cost

         B. Low maintenance

         C. _____

      II. Minivans (Caravan, Quest, Odyssey)

         A. Practical

         B. _____

         C. _____

      III. Luxury (Porsche, BMW, Mercedes, Lexus)

         A. High cost

            1. Initial

            2. _____

         B. _____

         C. Impressive features

1. _____

2. Unnecessary

∿ Examining Paragraphs of Classification

Student Writing

Here is an example of a student paragraph that demonstrates the steps for writing classification:

Subject:	doctors
Principle:	reasons for becoming a doctor
Classes:	financial, scientific, humanitarian

Doctors Have Their Symptoms, Too

Boris Belinsky

Topic sentence — Because I come from a large family that unfortunately has had a lot of illnesses, I have learned to classify doctors according to why they became doctors. <u>As doctors can diagnose illnesses by the symptoms they identify, I can figure out doctors' motives by their symptoms, by which I mean behavior</u>. Some doctors have chosen the field of medicine because they want to make

Support (class) — <u>money</u>. They hurry to visit their patients (customers) waiting in multiple office spaces, answer few questions, and never sit down. Although slow to respond to desperate phone calls, they are fast with the bills.

Support (class) — The second class is the group with <u>scientific</u> interests. Not as much concerned about money, they are often found in university hospitals, where they teach and work on special medical

Support (class)

problems. They may be a bit remote and explain symptoms in technical terms. The third group is my favorite: those who became doctors to <u>help people</u>. They spend much time with patients, often practice in areas that are not affluent, advocate preventative methods,

Concluding sentence

and do volunteer work. <u>Not all doctors easily fall into these three groups, but virtually every one has a tendency to do so.</u>

Professional Writing

*Styles of Leadership** [3rd-person POV]

William M. Pride, Robert J. Hughes, and Jack R. Kapoor

Written by three business professors, this paragraph is excerpted from a college textbook. It refers mainly to business institutions and the workplace, but it also covers all social units that depend on leadership, from the family to nations.

For many years, leadership was viewed as a combination of personality traits, such as self-confidence, concern for people, intelligence, and dependability. Achieving a consensus on which traits were most important was difficult, however, and attention turned to styles of leadership behavior. In the last few decades, several styles of leadership have been identified: authoritarian, laissez-faire, and democratic. The authoritarian leader holds all authority and responsibility, with communication usually moving from top to bottom. This leader assigns workers to specific tasks and expects orderly, precise results. The leaders at United Parcel Service employ authoritarian leadership. At the other extreme is the laissez-faire leader, who gives authority to employees. With the laissez-faire style, subordinates are allowed to work as they choose with a minimum of interference. Communication flows horizontally among group members. Leaders at Apple Computer are known to employ a laissez-faire leadership style in order to give employees as much freedom as possible to develop new products. The democratic leader holds final responsibility but also delegates authority to others, who participate

*Foundation of Business, Cengage Learning, 2008.

in determining work assignments. In this leadership style, communication is active both upward and downward. Employee commitment is high because of participation in the decision-making process. Managers for both Wal-Mart and Saturn have used the democratic leadership style to encourage employees to become more than just rank-and-file workers.

Exercise 3 Discussion and Critical Thinking

1. Underline the topic sentence.

2. What is the subject of this paragraph?

3. What is the principle that divides the subject into classes?

4. This paragraph explains the different styles of leadership without showing favor. Do you have a preferred style? If so, what is your preference and why?

Topics for Paragraphs of Classification

Most of these topics can also be used for short essays.

Reading-Based Writing Topic

See Chapter 5 for instruction and examples for writing summaries, reactions, and two-part responses (separate paragraphs of summary and reaction). Use quotations and references. Credit source(s).

"Styles of Leadership"

1. Write a reaction or a two-part response. In the reaction part, explain why you think that one style is best or that each one has its advantages or disadvantages, depending on the situation. Consider using examples from your experience.

Chapter 12 Classification: Establishing Groups

General Topics

2. Write a paragraph in which you classify a vocational group—lawyers, teachers, police officers, clergy, shop owners—according to their reasons for choosing their field: curiosity about or interest in the field, wanting to make money, or wanting to help others. For a helpful model on a similar topic, review "Doctors Have Their Symptoms, Too" on page 139.
3. Classify your pressures in different parts of your life as a college student.
4. Write a paragraph using one of the topics listed here. Divide your topic into groups according to a single principle.

   a. Drinkers
   b. Waitresses
   c. Dates
   d. Smiles
   e. TV watchers
   f. Sports fans
   g. Churchgoers
   h. Laughs
   i. Riders on buses or airplanes
   j. Rock music
   k. Beards
   l. Pet owners

Cross-Curricular Topic

5. Write a paragraph on one of the following terms:

   - Business: Types of real estate sales, banking, management styles, interviews, evaluations.
   - Geology: Types of rocks, earthquakes, mountains, rivers, erosion, faults
   - Biology: Types of cells, viruses, proteins, plants
   - Psychology: Types of stressors, aggression, adjustments, love
   - Sociology: Types of families, parents, deviants
   - Music: Types of instruments, singers, symphonies, operas, folk songs, rock, rap

Career-Related Topics

6. Discuss the different types of employees you have observed.
7. Discuss the different qualities of products or services in a particular field.
8. Discuss different types of customers with whom you have dealt (perhaps according to their purpose for seeking your services or products).

Writer's Guidelines at a Glance: Classification

1. Follow this procedure for writing paragraphs of classification:

   a. Select a plural subject.
   b. Decide on a principle for grouping the units of your subject.
   c. Establish the groups, or classes.
   d. Write about the classes.

2. Avoid uninteresting phrases for your classes, such as *good/average/bad*, *fast/medium/slow*, and *beautiful/ordinary/ugly*.
3. Avoid overlapping classes.
4. The Roman-numeral parts of your outline will probably indicate your classes.

   I. Class one
   II. Class two
   III. Class three

5. If you use subclasses, clearly indicate the different levels.
6. Following your outline, give somewhat equal (however much is appropriate) space to each class.
7. Consider using the Brandon Writing Process Worksheet with the Brandon Guide for Revising and Editing (see the form that can be enlarged and copied from inside the front of this book). Then, after your assignment is returned, update the Self-Evaluation Chart on the back of the front cover.

13

Comparison and Contrast: Showing Similarities and Differences

~ Writing Paragraphs of Comparison and Contrast

Comparison and contrast is a method of showing similarities and dissimilarities between subjects. Comparison is concerned with organizing and developing points of similarity; contrast has the same function for dissimilarity. Sometimes a writing assignment may require that you cover only similarities or only dissimilarities. Occasionally, an instructor may ask you to separate one from the other. Usually, you will combine them. For convenience, the term *comparison* is often applied to both comparison and contrast because both use the same techniques and are frequently combined into one operation.

Generating Topics and Working with the 4 *P*'s

Comparison and contrast is basic to your thinking. In your daily activities, you consider similarities and dissimilarities among persons, things, concepts, political leaders, doctors, friends, instructors, schools, nations, classes, movies, and so on. You naturally turn to comparison and contrast to solve problems and to make decisions in your affairs and in your writing. Because you have had so many comparative experiences, finding a topic to write about is likely to be only a matter of choosing from a great number of appealing ideas. Freewriting, brainstorming, and clustering will help you generate topics that are especially workable and appropriate for particular assignments.

144

Many college writing assignments will specify a topic or ask you to choose one from a list. Regardless of the source of your topic, the procedure for developing your ideas by comparison and contrast is the same as the procedure for developing topics of your own choosing. That procedure can be appropriately called the 4 *P*'s: **p**urpose, **p**oints, **p**atterns, and **p**resentation.

Purpose

Are you trying to show relationships (how things are similar and dissimilar) or to show that one side is better (ranking)? If you want to show that one actor, one movie, one writer, one president, one product, or one idea is better than another, your purpose is to persuade. You will emphasize the superiority of one side over the other in your topic sentence and in your support.

If you want to explain something about a topic by showing each subject in relation to others, then your purpose is informative. For example, you might be comparing two composers, Beethoven and Mozart. Both were musical geniuses, so you then decide it would be senseless to argue that one is superior to the other. Instead, you choose to reveal interesting information about both by showing them in relation to each other.

You may have heard people talk about puppy love and true love and now you decide to explore those two varieties as a topic for a comparative study. Your purpose would be to explain that puppy love and true love are different.

Points

Continuing with the example of two types of love, you would come up with a list of ideas, or points, that you could apply somewhat equally to the two types. From the list, you would select two or three and circle them.

(passion)

intimacy

(age of lovers)

commitment
duration

(circumstances)

Patterns

You then would need to organize your material according to the two basic patterns: subject by subject and point by point. The **subject-by-subject pattern** presents all of one side and then all of the other side.

I. Puppy love
   A. Passion
   B. Intimacy
   C. Commitment

II. True love
   A. Passion
   B. Intimacy
   C. Commitment

The **point-by-point pattern** shows the points in relation to the sides (subjects) one at a time. This is the more common pattern.

I. Passion
   A. Puppy love
      1. Consuming
      2. Intense
   B. True love
      1. Present
      2. Proportional

II. Intimacy
   A. Puppy love
      1. Lots of talking
      2. Superficial
   B. True love
      1. Good communication
         a. Feelings
         b. Ideas
      2. Deep

III. Commitment
   A. Puppy love
      1. Not tested
      2. Weak, if at all
   B. True love
      1. Proven
      2. Profound

Presentation

Here you would use your outline (or cluster list) to begin writing your paragraph. You would use appropriate explanations, details, and examples for support. See page 148 for a final draft of this topic in the point-by-point pattern.

Transitional Words

Consider using the following transitional words to improve coherence by connecting ideas with ideas, sentences with sentences, and paragraphs with paragraphs:

- **FOR COMPARISON AND CONTRAST: Comparison:** *in the same way, similarly, likewise, also, by comparison, in a like manner, as, with, as though, both, like, just as*

- **Contrast:** *but, by contrast, in contrast, despite, however, instead, nevertheless, on (to) the contrary, in spite of, still, yet, unlike, even so, rather than, otherwise*

~ Practicing Patterns of Comparison and Contrast

Exercise 1 Practicing Patterns

Fill in the blanks in the following outlines to complete the comparisons and contrasts.

Subject-by-Subject Pattern

1. Friends: Marla and Justine

    I. Marla

       A. Appearance

       B. _____

       C. _____

    II. Justine

       A. _____

       B. Personality

       C. _____

Point-by-Point Pattern

2. Two bosses: Mr. Santo and Ms. Elliott
   I. Disposition
      A. Mr. Santo
      B. Ms. Elliott

   II. Knowledge of _____
      A. _____
      B. Ms. Elliott

   III. _____
      A. Mr. Santo
      B. _____

〰 Examining Paragraphs of Comparison and Contrast

Student Writing

Two Loves: Puppy and True **[3rd-person POV]**

Jennifer Jeffries

Jennifer Jeffries considered several topics before she selected different kinds of love. Just a bit of freewriting convinced her that she had the information and interest to do a good job. In a psychology course she had recently taken, she studied the topic of love, and here she does a variation on a theory by R. J. Sternberg. She submitted a copy of Sternberg's theory with her paragraph.

Topic sentence	Of the several forms of love, the two opposite extremes are puppy love and true love. If love in its fullest form has three parts—passion, intimacy, and commitment—then puppy love and true love could be called *incomplete* and *complete*, respectively.
Point	Passion is common to both. Puppy love couldn't exist without *passion*, hence the word *puppy*—an immature animal that jumps around excitedly licking somebody's face.

Subject A	A person in puppy love is attracted physically to someone and is constantly aroused. A
Subject B	person in true love is also passionate, but the passion is proportional to other parts of love and life. True-love passion is based on more than physical attraction, though that should not be discounted. It is with
Point	the intimacy factor that puppy love really
Subject A	begins to differ from true love. Puppy love may promote a lot of talk, but most of it can be attributed to the arousal factor. There's no closeness and depth of shared
Subject B	experience. But with true love there is a genuine closeness and shared concern for each other that is supportive and reassuring. That closeness usually comes from years of shared experience, which also proves commitment.
Point	And it is just that factor, the commitment, that is probably the main difference between
Subject A	puppy love and true love. The people in puppy love may talk about eternity, but their love hasn't really gotten outside the physical realm. Their love has not been tested, whereas those in true love have a proven
Subject B	commitment. True love has survived troubles in this imperfect world and become stronger. And it has survived because it has more than the one dimension. These considerations show that these two loves are very different, though puppy love may, with time, become true love. That possibility doesn't mean that age necessarily corresponds with one form of love. A person of any age can, by knowing passion, intimacy, and commitment, experience true love, but true love is more likely to develop over a period of time.

Exercise 2   Discussion and Critical Thinking

1. Do you agree with Jeffries's decision to use the point-by-point pattern rather than the subject-by-subject one? Why or why not?

2. Jeffries says that puppy love can become true love. Can true love ever become puppy love? Discuss.

3. Jeffries implies that one is much more likely to fall out of puppy love than true love. Do you agree? Why or why not?

4. How much time is required for true love to develop? Explain.

Professional Writing

*Public and Private**

Richard Rodriguez

> *Every person has a public life and a private life, and the character of each is colored by a variety of cultural forces. If the family in the United States includes parents born in Mexico, then the public life may be conducted mainly in English and the private life mainly in Spanish. In this passage from his book* Hunger of Memory: The Education of Richard Rodriguez. *Rodriguez says cultural contrast is natural and even complementary.*

For me there were none of the gradations between public and private society so normal to a maturing child. Outside the house

*From Richard Rodriguez, *Hunger of Memory: The Education of Richard Rodriguez* (Bantam Books, 1982).

was public society; inside the house was private. Just opening or
closing the screen door behind me was an important experience.
I'd rarely leave home all alone or without reluctance. Walking
down the sidewalk, under the canopy of tall trees, I'd warily
notice the—suddenly—silent neighborhood kids who stood
warily watching me. Nervously, I'd arrive at the grocery store to
hear there the sounds of the gringo—foreign to me—reminding
me that in this world so big, I was a foreigner. But then I'd return. Walking back toward our house, climbing the steps from
the sidewalk, when the front door was open in summer, I'd hear
voices beyond the screen door talking in Spanish. For a second or
two, I'd stay, linger there, listening. Smiling, I'd hear my mother
call out, saying in Spanish (words), "Is that you, Richard?" all
the while her sounds would assure me: You are home now;
come closer; inside. With us.

Exercise 3   Discussion and Critical Thinking

1. What is the topic sentence of this paragraph?

2. What sounds especially remind Rodriguez of the separation
   between private and public society?

3. What part of the house separates public and private society?

4. Is the pattern used in this paragraph point by point or subject
   by subject?

5. Is this separation of public and private society present in most families, regardless of ethnic considerations? Explain with reference to a family you know.

Blue as in Boy, *Pink as in* Girl* [3rd-person POV]

Sharon S. Brehm

This paragraph comes from "Stereotypes, Prejudices, and Discrimination," a chapter in Social Psychology, *a college textbook by Sharon S. Brehm. Comparing males and females, she maintains that discrimination based on gender begins at birth and never stops.*

When a baby is born, the first words uttered ring loud and clear: "It's a boy!" or "It's a girl!" In many hospitals, the newborn boy immediately is given a blue hat and the newborn girl a pink hat. The infant receives a gender-appropriate name and is showered with gender-appropriate gifts. Over the next few years, the typical boy is supplied with toy trucks, baseballs, pretend tools, guns, and chemistry sets; the typical girl is furnished with dolls, stuffed animals, pretend make-up kits, kitchen sets, and tea sets. As they enter school, many expect the boy to earn money by delivering newspapers and to enjoy math and computers, while they expect the girl to babysit and to enjoy crafts, music, and social activities. These distinctions persist in college, as more male students major in economics and the sciences and more female students in the arts, languages, and humanities. In the work force, more men become doctors, construction workers, auto mechanics, airplane pilots, investment bankers, and engineers. In contrast, more women become secretaries, schoolteachers, nurses, flight attendants, bank tellers, and housewives. Back on the home front, the life cycle begins again when a man and woman have their first baby and discover that "It's a girl!" or "It's a boy!" The traditional pinks and blues are not as distinct as they used

*From Sharon S. Brehm, *Social Psychology* 5e. © 2002 Wadsworth, a part of Cengage Learning, Inc. Reproduced by permission. www.cengage.com/permissions.

to be. Many gender barriers of the past have been broken down, and the colors have somewhat blended together. Nevertheless, **sexism**—prejudice and discrimination based on a person's gender—still exists. Indeed, it begins with the fact that sex is the most conspicuous social category we use to identify ourselves and others.

Exercise 4   Discussion and Critical Thinking

1. What are the subject and focus parts of the topic sentence? *Hint:* The topic sentence is toward the end of the paragraph.

2. Is Brehm trying mainly to inform, to persuade, or to do both? Explain.

3. Is this paragraph more comparison or more contrast? Give evidence.

4. What points does Brehm use?

5. Does Brehm use the alternating or the opposing pattern?

6. Given a choice, would girls naturally choose dolls and boys trucks? In other words, are boys and girls just genetically different in that respect? Discuss.

7. Does your experience tell you that Brehm is right or wrong? If she is right, would you use the terms "prejudice" and "discrimination" to characterize the situation? If she is correct, how would one explain the statistical fact that, overall, for the current generation, females are better educated than men?

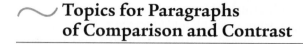

Topics for Paragraphs of Comparison and Contrast

Most of these topics can also be used for short essays.

Reading-Based Writing Topics

See Chapter 5 for instruction and examples for writing summaries, reactions, and two-part responses (separate paragraphs of summary and reaction). Use quotations and references. Credit source(s).

"Two Loves: Puppy and True"

1. Using the terms from this paragraph, write a comparison-and-contrast paragraph on a puppy-love couple and a true-love couple you know. Your subject could be one couple at different stages of their relationship.

"Public and Private"

2. Write a reaction in which you discuss the idea that all family members have a private world and a public world. What dimension is different when there is a cultural and language difference? Apply your opinions to what you have observed and experienced. Concentrate on one family that you compare and contrast with the family in Rodriguez's life. Refer directly to and quote from his paragraph.

"Blue as in *Boy*, Pink as in *Girl*"

3. Write a paragraph patterned on three or more of the main points of this reading selection—colors, names, toys, activities, college majors, careers—in which you discuss your own family or another family you know well with attention to at least one male child and one female child. Comment on the discrimination that does occur. Be sure to use references to and quotations from this source.

General Topic

4. Select a general subject from the following list and write a comparison-and-contrast paragraph. Provide specific names and other detailed information as you develop your ideas by using the 4 *P*'s (purpose, points, patterns, and presentation).

   a. Two automobiles
   b. Two fast-food restaurants

   c. Two homes
   d. Two people who play the same sport
   e. Two generations
   f. Two motorcycles, cars, or snowmobiles
   g. Two actors, singers, or musicians
   h. Two ways of learning
   i. Two ways of controlling
   j. Two kinds of child care
   k. Two mothers: one who stays at home and one who works outside the home

Cross-Curricular Topics

5. In the fields of nutritional science and health, compare and contrast two diets, two exercise programs, or two pieces of exercise equipment.
6. Compare and contrast your field of study (or one aspect of it) as it existed some time ago (specify the years) and as it is now. Refer to new developments and discoveries, such as scientific breakthroughs and technological advances.

Career-Related Topics

7. Compare and contrast two products or services, with the purpose of showing that one is better.
8. Compare and contrast two management styles or two work styles.
9. Compare and contrast two career fields to show that one is better for you.
10. Compare and contrast a public school and a business.
11. Compare and contrast an athletic team and a business.

Writer's Guidelines at a Glance: Comparison and Contrast

1. Work with the 4 *P*'s:

 - **Purpose:** Decide whether you want to inform (show relationships) or to persuade (show that one side is better).
 - **Points:** Decide which ideas you will apply to each side. Consider beginning by making a list from which to select.

- **Patterns:** Decide whether to use subject-by-subject or point-by-point organization.
- **Presentation:** Decide to what extent you should develop your ideas. Be sure to use cross-references to make connections and to use examples and details to support your views.

2. Your basic subject-by-subject outline will probably look like this:

    I. Subject 1
      A. Point 1
      B. Point 2

   II. Subject 2
      A. Point 1
      B. Point 2

3. Your basic point-by-point outline will probably look like this:

    I. Point 1
      A. Subject 1
      B. Subject 2

   II. Point 2
      A. Subject 1
      B. Subject 2

4. Consider using the Brandon Writing Process Worksheet with the Brandon Guide for Revising and Editing (see the form that can be enlarged and copied from inside the front of this book). Then, after your assignment is returned, update the Self-Evaluation Chart on the back of the front cover.

14

Definition:
Clarifying Terms

～ Writing Paragraphs of Definition

Most definitions are short; they consist of a **synonym** (a word that has the same meaning as the term to be defined), a phrase, or a sentence. For example, we might say that a hypocrite is a person "professing beliefs or virtues he or she does not possess." But terms can also be defined by **etymology**, or word history. *Hypocrite* once meant "actor" (*hypocrites*) in Greek because an actor was pretending to be someone else. Although we may find this information interesting and revealing, the history of a word may be of limited use because the meaning has changed drastically over the years. Sometimes definitions occupy a paragraph or an entire essay. The short definition is called a **simple definition**; the longer one is known as an **extended definition**.

Techniques for Development

Paragraphs of definition can take many forms. Among the more common techniques for writing a paragraph of definition are the patterns we have worked with in previous chapters. Consider each of those patterns when you need to write an extended definition. For a particular term, some forms will be more useful than others; use the pattern that best fulfills your purpose.

Each of the following questions takes a pattern of writing and directs it toward definition.

- **Narration:** Can I tell an anecdote or a story to define this subject (such as *jerk, humanitarian,* or *patriot*)? This form may overlap with description and exemplification.
- **Description:** Can I describe this subject (such as *a whale* or *the moon*)?

- **Exemplification:** Can I give examples of this subject (such as naming individuals to provide examples of *actors, diplomats,* or *satirists*)?
- **Analysis by division:** Can I divide this subject into parts (for example, the parts of *a heart, a cell,* or *a carburetor*)?
- **Process analysis:** Can I define this subject (such as *lasagna, a tornado, a hurricane, blood pressure,* or any number of scientific processes) by describing how to make it or how it occurs? Common to the methodology of communicating in science, this approach is sometimes called the "operational definition."
- **Cause and effect:** Can I define this subject (such as *a flood, a drought, a riot,* or *a cancer*) by its causes and effects?
- **Classification:** Can I group this subject (such as kinds of *families, cultures, religions,* or *governments*) into classes?

Subject	Class	Characteristics
A republic	is a form of government	in which power resides in the people (the electorate).

- **Comparison and contrast:** Can I define this subject (such as *extremist* or *patriot*) by explaining what it is similar to and different from? If you are defining *orangutan* for a person who has never heard of one but has heard of the gorilla, then you could make comparison-and-contrast statements. If you want to define *patriot,* you might want to stress what it is not (the contrast) before you explain what it is: A patriot is not a one-dimensional flag waver, not someone who hates "foreigners" because America is always right and always best.

When you develop ideas for a definition paragraph, use a cluster to consider all the paragraph patterns you have learned. Put a double bubble around the subject to be defined. Then put a single bubble around the paragraph patterns and add appropriate words. If a paragraph pattern is not relevant to what you are defining, leave it blank. If you want to expand your range of information, you could add a bubble for a simple dictionary definition and another for an etymological definition. The bubble cluster on page 159 shows how a term could be defined using different paragraph patterns.

Order

The organization of your extended definition is likely to be one of emphasis, but it may be space or time, depending on the subject material. You may use just one pattern of development for the overall sequence. Use the principles of organization discussed in previous chapters.

Introduction and Development

Consider these ways of introducing a definition: with a question, with a statement of what the subject is not, with a statement of what the word or phrase originally meant, or with a discussion of why a clear definition is important. You may use a combination of these ways or all of them before you continue with your definition.

Development, whether in the form of sentences for the paragraph or of paragraphs for the essay, is likely to represent one or more of the patterns of narration, description, exposition (with its own subdivisions), and argumentation.

Whether you personalize a definition depends on your purpose and your audience. Your instructor may ask you to write about a word within the context of your experience or to write about it from a detached, clinical viewpoint.

Transitional Words

Consider using the following transitional words to improve coherence by connecting ideas with ideas, sentences with sentences, and paragraphs with paragraphs:

- **FOR DEFINITION:** *originates from, means, derives from, refers to, for example, as a term, as a concept, label, similar to, different from, in a particular context, in common usage, in historical context*

◯ Practicing Patterns of Definition

Exercise 1   Completing Patterns

Fill in the following double bubble with a term to be defined. You might want to define culturally diverse society, educated person, leader, role model, friend, success, *or* intelligence. *Then fill in at least one more bubble on the right for each paragraph pattern. If the pattern does not apply (that is, if it would not provide useful information for your definition), mark it NA ("not applicable").*

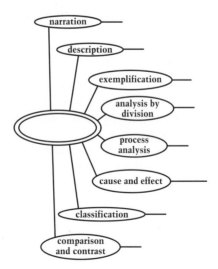

～ Examining Patterns of Definition

Student Writing

Going Too Far **[3rd-person POV—or is it?]**

Linda Wong

After hearing people say, "I just can't love him [or her] enough" and also "It was too much of a good thing," Linda Wong set out to explore the definition of the word extremist.

What the term does not mean

Simple definition

Topic sentence

Example/ contrast

Example/ contrast

Example/ contrast

Some people believe that it is good to be an extremist in some areas, but those people are actually changing the meaning of the word. According to the *Random House Dictionary of the English Language*, the word *extremism* itself means "excessively biased ideas, intemperate conduct." The extremist goes too far; that means going too far in whatever the person is doing. I once heard someone say that it is good for people to be extremists in love. But that is not true. It is good to be enthusiastically and sincerely in love, but extremists in love love excessively and intemperately. People who love well may be tender and sensitive and attentive, but extremists are possessive or smothering. The same can be said of parents. We all want to be good parents, but parental extremists involve themselves too much in the lives of their children, who, in turn, may find it difficult to develop as individuals and become independent. Even in patriotism, good patriots are to be distinguished from extreme patriots. Good patriots love their country, but extreme patriots love their country so much that

they think citizens from other countries
are inferior and suspect. Extreme patriots
may have Hitler-like tendencies. Just what
is wrong with extremists then? It is the

Examples   loss of perspective. The extremists are
so preoccupied with one concern that they
lose their sense of balance. They are the
workaholics, the zealots, the superpatriots
of the world. They may begin with a good
objective, but they focus on it so much that
they can become destructive, obnoxious, and

Effect and   often pitiful. The worst effect is that these
concluding   extremists lose their completeness as human
sentence   beings.

Exercise 2 Discussion and Critical Thinking

1. Wong says that extremists "can become destructive, obnoxious,
   and often pitiful." Can you think of any good effects from people
   who are extremists? For example, what about a scientist who
   works fifteen hours a day to find a cure for a horrible disease?
   Is it possible that the scientist may succeed in his or her profession and fail in his or her personal life? But what if the scientist
   does not want a personal life? Discuss.

2. Why does Wong use contrast so much?

3. According to Wong, would it be bad for a person to be an
   extremist in religion? Discuss.

Prison Slang **[3rd-person POV]**

Ruby Red

Because prison is a unique community with edgy and tenuous relationships, it is predictable that it would have its own variety of language. For student Ruby Red (a pseudonym), knowing prison slang is crucial to her well-being.

Topic sentence and basic definition	Prison slang is like other slang in that it is language that is used in a special way for special reasons. Like conventional slang, some words have unusual, nonstandard
Comparison	meanings, and some words are invented. Most slang is used by people who want to conform to group language customs. In prison it is used both by people who don't want others to know what they are talking about and by those
More basic definition	who are seeking group identity. As a variety of language, it is like a dialect because it is just part of the culture of that
Classification (areas)	group. Prison slang covers many areas, but it especially reflects prisoners' concerns: violence, talking, and reputation. The very
Examples follow	idea of violence is strangely muted by the terms used to discuss brutal acts. If a person is attacked by a group of people who throw a blanket over her head before they beat her, she is said to be the recipient of a "blanket party" given by a "rat pack." If she "caught a cold" or they "took her wind," she died. They may have killed her with a sharp instrument called a "shank" or a "shiv." Perhaps she didn't know there was a "raven" (contract) out on her; she thought they were only "putting on a floor show" (pretending) or "selling wolf tickets" (bluffing). She should have listened to their talk more carefully. They said she had "snitched them

off" (informed), and her friend had "pulled
her coat" (told her something she should
know), but then a cop came by and she said,
"Radio it, dog-face it, dummy up" (all
meaning "shut up"), and then she "put it on
hold" (filed it away for future use). That
was her mistake because the woman out to get
her was a "die hard, hard core, cold piece"
(each meaning "career criminal"), who was a
"hog" (enforcer), "dancer" (fighter), and a

Concluding "jive bitch" (agitator). <u>These are only a few</u>
statement   <u>of the hundreds of slang words used by women</u>
<u>behind bars. They are an important part of</u>
<u>prison life</u>.

Exercise 3   Discussion and Critical Thinking

1. The paragraph begins with a topic sentence and a basic definition. What form (topic sentence and support, or topic sentence,
   support, and concluding sentence) does it take?

2. How is prison slang actually an integral part of the culture?

3. With what is prison slang compared? Is that a valid and useful
   comparison? Discuss.

4. What is the main pattern (narration, description, exemplification,
   analysis by division, cause and effect, classification) used in
   explaining prison slang?

5. What other patterns are used?

6. How are examples grouped, or classified?

7. After reading this paragraph carefully, do you think of prison as a place of constant tension and violence or as a complex society with many concerns?

Professional Writing

Burnout [3rd-person POV]

Gregory Moorhead and Ricky W. Griffin

Occupational sociologists Gregory Moorhead and Ricky W. Griffin provide the following definition of burnout adapted from their book Organizational Behavior *(Cengage Learning, 2009). Their definition pertains mainly to vocational work, but burnout can occur in any organization—church, government, recreation, even marriage and family.*

Burnout, a consequence of stress, has clear implications for both people and organizations. Burnout is a general feeling of exhaustion that develops when a person simultaneously experiences too much pressure and has too few sources of satisfaction. Burnout usually develops in the following way. First, people with high aspirations and strong motivation to get things done are prime candidates for burnout under certain conditions. They are especially vulnerable when the organization suppresses or limits their initiative while constantly demanding that they serve the organization's own ends. In such a situation, the individual is likely to put too much of himself or herself into the job. In other words, the person may well keep trying to meet his or her own agenda while simultaneously trying to fulfill the organization's expectations. The most likely effects of this situation are prolonged stress, fatigue, frustration, and helplessness under the burden of overwhelming demands. The person literally exhausts his or her aspiration and motivation, much as a candle burns itself out. Loss of self-confidence and psychological withdrawal follow. Ultimately, burnout results. At this point, the individual may start dreading going to work in the morning, may put in longer hours but accomplish less than before, and may generally display mental and physical exhaustion.

Exercise 4　Discussion and Critical Thinking

1. Does the first sentence or the second sentence provide a better definition? Which one is the topic sentence for the paragraph? What are the subject and the focus parts of the topic sentence?

2. What other pattern—comparison and contrast, classification, cause and effect, or narration—provides structure for this definition? Explain.

3. If you were going to personalize this definition, what other pattern(s) would you use? Explain.

～ Topics for Paragraphs of Definition

Most of these topics can also be used for short essays.

Reading-Based Writing Topics

See Chapter 5 for instruction and examples for writing summaries, reactions, and two-part responses (separate paragraphs of summary and reaction). Use quotations and references. Credit source(s).

"Going Too Far"

1. Apply the definition of *extremist* from Linda Wong's paragraph to a situation you are familiar with: an overprotective parent, a controlling companion, an overly controlling boss, a too-strict police officer or teacher, a too-virtuous friend, a preacher, a too-clean housekeeper (companion, parent), a zealous patriot, a

person fanatical about a diet, a person concerned too much with good health or exercise. You might begin your paragraph with the statement: "Nothing is good when carried to the extreme." Or "It is good to be _____, but when _____ is carried to the extreme, the result is _____."

"Burnout"

2. Borrow the definition of *burnout* from this paragraph (but give credit) and develop it with an extended example of someone you know who is or was a burnout. The definition is likely to be developed as a narrative around a set of causes and effects. Think of those who may be temporarily or terminally burned out—those drained of enthusiasm, feeling, and direction and those reduced to shambling, hollow-eyed hulks: bosses, workers, teachers and students, parents and offspring, young and old. Perhaps you would like to write about a person who seemed clinically burned out but then experienced a rekindling of flames of enthusiasm, in a positive sense. If so, who or what lit the fire? Use references and quotations.

General Topics

3. Write a definition of "_____ slang." That variety of slang comes from a generation (your generation, especially of your social group), a blend of English and another language (such as Spanish and English—Spanglish; Chinese and English—Chineselish), a gang, a work-centered group (jargon), or a men's prison. Use numerous examples. Consider organizing your definition around various situations in which the slang would be used. For a useful model definition on a similar subject, review "Prison Slang" on page 163.
4. Write an extended definition about one of the following terms:
   a. Workaholic
   b. Sexist
   c. Liberated woman
   d. Sexual harassment
   e. Macho
   f. Soul food, ethnic food (any one), fast food, McFood
   g. Form of music, such as rockabilly, hip-hop, rap, techno, punk
   h. Street smart, school smart, sports smart, work smart, party smart

Cross-Curricular Topic

5. Define one of the following terms in a paragraph:

   a. History and government: socialism, democracy, patriotism, capitalism, communism
   b. Philosophy: existentialism, free will, determinism, ethics, stoicism
   c. Education: charter schools, school choice, gifted program, ESL (English as a second language), paired teaching, digital school
   d. Music: symphony, sonata, orchestra, tonic systems
   e. Health science: autism, circulatory system, respiratory system, thyroid, cancer, herbal remedies, acupuncture
   f. Marketing: depression, digitalization, discretionary income, electronic commerce, globalization, marketing channel, free trade, telemarketing, warehouse clubs

Career-Related Topic

6. Define one of the following terms by using the appropriate pattern(s) of development (such as exemplification, cause and effect, narration, comparison and contrast, description, analysis by division, and process analysis): *total quality management, quality control, downsizing, outsourcing, business ethics, customer satisfaction, cost effectiveness.*

Writer's Guidelines at a Glance: Definition

1. Use clustering to consider other patterns of development that may be used to define your term.
2. The organization of your extended definition is likely to be one of emphasis, but it may be space or time, depending on the subject. You may use just one pattern of development for the overall organization.
3. Consider these ways of introducing a definition: with a question, with a statement of what the subject is not, with a statement of what the word or phrase originally meant, or with a discussion of why a clear definition is important. You may use a combination of these ways before you continue with your definition.

4. Whether you personalize a definition depends on your purpose and your audience. Your instructor may ask you to write about a word within the context of your own experience or to write about it from a detached, clinical viewpoint.

5. Consider using the Brandon Writing Process Worksheet with the Brandon Guide for Revising and Editing (see the form that can be enlarged and copied from inside the front of this book). Then, after your assignment is returned, update the Self-Evaluation Chart on the back of the front cover.

15

Argument:
Writing to Influence

~ Writing Paragraphs of Argument

Persuasion and Argument Defined

Persuasion is a broad term; when we persuade, we try to influence people to think in a certain way or to do something. **Argument** is persuasion on a topic about which reasonable people disagree. Argument involves controversy. Whereas exercising appropriately is probably not controversial because reasonable people do not dispute the idea, an issue such as gun control is controversial. In this chapter, we will be concerned mainly with the kind of persuasion that involves argument.

Components of Your Paragraph

Statements of argument are informal or formal in design. Although an opinion column in a newspaper is likely to have little set structure, an argument in college writing is likely to be tightly organized. Nevertheless, the opinion column and the college paper have much in common. Both provide a proposition, which is the main point of the argument, and both provide support, which is the evidence or the reasons that back up the proposition.

For a well-structured paragraph, an organizational plan is desirable. When you write a paragraph of argument, consider these elements: background, proposition, qualification of proposition, refutation, and support. Ask yourself the following questions as you develop your ideas:

- **Background:** What is the historical or social context for this controversial issue?
- **Proposition** (the **topic sentence** of a paragraph of argument): What do I want my audience to believe or to do?

170

- **Qualification of proposition:** Can I limit my proposition so that those who disagree cannot easily challenge me with exceptions? If, for example, I am in favor of using animals for scientific experimentation, am I concerned only with medical experiments or with any use, including that pertaining to the cosmetic industry?
- **Refutation** (taking the opposing view into account, mainly to point out its fundamental weakness): What is the view on the other side, and why is it flawed in reasoning or evidence?
- **Support:** In addition to sound reasoning, can I use appropriate facts, examples, statistics, and opinions of authorities?

The basic form for a paragraph of argument includes the proposition (the topic sentence) and support. The support sentences are, in effect, *because* statements; that is, the proposition is valid *because* of the support. Your organization should look something like this:

> *Proposition (topic sentence):* It is time to pass a national law restricting smoking in public places.
>
>   I. Discomfort of the nonsmoker (support 1)
>   II. Health of the nonsmoker (support 2)
> III. Cost to the nation (support 3)

Kinds of Evidence

In addition to sound reasoning, you can use the following kinds of evidence, or support.

1. **Facts.** Martin Luther King Jr. was killed in Memphis, Tennessee, on April 4, 1968. Because an event that has happened is true and can be verified, this statement about King is a fact. But that James Earl Ray acted alone in killing King is to some a questionable fact. That King was the greatest of all civil rights leaders is also opinion because that statement cannot be verified.

   Some facts are readily accepted because they are general knowledge—you and your reader know them to be true because they can be or have been verified. Other "facts" are based on personal observation and are reported in various publications but may be false or questionable. You should always be concerned about the reliability of the source for both the information you use and the information used by those with other viewpoints. Still other so-called facts are genuinely debatable because of their complexity or the incompleteness of the knowledge available.
2. **Examples.** You must present a sufficient number of examples, and the examples must be relevant.

3. **Statistics.** Statistics are facts and data of a numerical kind that are classified and tabulated to present significant information about a given subject.

   Avoid presenting a long list of figures; select statistics carefully and relate them to things familiar to your reader. The millions of dollars spent on a war in a single week, for example, become more comprehensible when expressed in terms of what the money would purchase in education, highways, or urban renewal.

   To test the validity of statistics, either yours or your opponent's, ask: Who gathered the statistics? Under what conditions? For what purpose? How are they used?
4. **Evidence from, and opinions of, authorities.** Most readers accept facts from recognized, reliable sources—government publications, standard reference works, and books and periodicals published by established firms. In addition, readers will accept evidence and opinions from individuals who, because of their knowledge and experience, are recognized as experts.

   In using authoritative sources as proof, keep these points in mind:

   - Select authorities who are generally recognized as experts in their field.
   - Use authorities who qualify in the field pertinent to your argument.
   - Select authorities whose views are not biased.
   - Try to use several authorities.
   - Identify an authority's credentials clearly in your paragraph.

Transitional Words

Consider using the following transitional words to improve coherence by connecting ideas with ideas, sentences with sentences, and paragraphs with paragraphs:

- **FOR ARGUMENT:** *it follows that, as a result, causes taken collectively, as a concession, even though, of course, in the context of, in the light of, in the final analysis, following this, further, as additional support, moreover, consequently, according to, in support of, contrary to, therefore, naturally*

◠ Practicing Patterns of Argument

Exercise 1 Completing Patterns

Fill in the blanks in the following outlines with supporting statements for each proposition. Each outline uses this pattern:

Proposition
  I. Support
 II. Support
III. Support

1. Proposition: College athletes should be paid.

   I. _____

  II. They work long hours in practice and competition.

 III. They have less time than many other students for study.

2. Proposition: Zoos are beneficial institutions.

   I. _____

  II. They preserve endangered species by captive breeding.

 III. They study animal diseases and find cures.

◠ Examining Paragraphs of Argument

Student Writing

My Life to Live—or Not **[3rd-person POV]**
Angela DeSarro

After Angela DeSarro received a list of topics from which to select, she went to the library to obtain some information about the ones that interested her. One such topic was euthanasia. Her electronic data bank offered her an essay in the Journal of the American Medical Association *about a doctor who illegally assisted a suffering, terminally ill patient. DeSarro's mind and emotions came together on the issue and she had her topic.*

Debbie, 20, was dying of ovarian cancer.
Racked with pain, nauseous and emaciated,
she sought the ultimate relief and found it

Proposition

in euthanasia. A doctor administered a drug and she died. It was a hidden, secret act. It was also illegal in Debbie's state, but this case was written up in the *Journal of the American Medical Association*. <u>Surely the time has come for a nationwide law legalizing this practice under specific provisions and regulations</u>. Debbie had reached the point

Support

of not only <u>enduring terrible pain</u> but of <u>vomiting constantly</u> and <u>not being able to sleep</u>. <u>Pain-killing medication no longer worked</u>. She wanted to die with what she regarded as a degree of dignity. She had already become a withered, suffering human being with tubes coming out of her nose, throat, and urinary tract, and she was losing

Support

all self-control. <u>She also believed that it should be up to her, under these conditions, to decide when and how she should die</u>. Laws in most places prohibit terminally ill patients from choosing death and physicians from assisting them. One state, Oregon, has a law favoring physician-assisted suicide, at least in the limited cases of terminally ill people expected to live less than six months.

Concluding sentence as a restated proposition

Numerous people have benefited from that law; it was not abused. <u>It, or a similar form, should be enacted nationwide</u>.

Exercise 2 Discussion and Critical Thinking

1. What kinds of evidence (facts, example or examples, statement by expert) does DeSarro use to support her argument?

2. What might be the objections to DeSarro's reasoned argument?

3. Do you agree or disagree with DeSarro's argument? Why?

Chick-O-Stick Forever! **[3rd-person POV]**
Martin Bradley

For one suggestion for topics, students were encouraged to argue that a specific product is superior to others in the same group. Martin Bradley selected his long-time favorite from the food group pertaining to candy.

Snickers, Butterfinger, Skittles—the list of favorite junk candies goes on for miles, but most people have not even heard of the best candy treat ever invented. It's an oldie— invented in 1938, as a matter of fact. The most striking thing about this candy is its utter lack of chocolate. Instead, the outside is covered in coconut. Even more striking perhaps is that this thing is not rectangular. It is cylindrical, it is approximately eight inches long, and it tastes something like the inside of a Butterfinger, but oh, so much better without the low quality pseudo-chocolate covering. Kids in the '50s and '60s loved these things, but the Chick-O-Stick never reached the stratospheric heights of popularity that other mass-produced confections have enjoyed. One can attribute its cult candy status and its "hip factor" to an absolute lack of advertisement. People just have to find out about this candy "on the streets" from true candy aficionados. Another thing that makes the Chick-O-Stick special is the rarity factor. These things are not available just anywhere. One must hunt for this treat among liquor stores, independent gas stations, and other places where "retro" candies can be purchased, and once the quarry has been found, the real selection process begins. As any Chick-O-Stick lover knows, this is a fragile candy prone to cracking into smaller sections. Unacceptable! The Chick-O-Stick must be unfractured; otherwise, the flavor leaks out! Once the perfect specimen has been located, the extensive search process becomes unimportant, for the flavor party begins. When someone first bites into one of these delicious confections, a question inevitably follows: "How come I haven't heard of these before?" The answer is that some things are too good to advertise. If something is good, it doesn't need to be advertised. Besides, one must find candy enlightenment on his or her own. Now, go seek ultimate candy knowledge.

Exercise 3   Discussion and Critical Thinking

1. What does Bradley say are the qualities that make Chick-O-Stick the most underrated candy bar?

2. Of the qualities discussed by Bradley, which can be argued on the basis of evidence rather than opinion?

3. How compelling is Bradley's argument?

4. What is your favorite candy bar? How would you make a case that it is better than Bradley's?

Professional Writing

A Modest Proposal: Guys Shouldn't Drive Till 25 [3rd-person POV]

Joyce Gallagher

> *Freelance writer Joyce Gallagher says we should look at the national problem of motor vehicle accidents and apply the brakes. To Gallagher, statistics tell the story, and the solution is as inevitable to her as it may be unthinkable to you.*

In the year 2001, 57,480 people were killed in motor vehicle accidents.* That figure is within a few hundred of being the same number as those killed in the Vietnam War. We took drastic measures back in the early 1970s and ended that war in a way shocking to some: we left. The time has come for another drastic scheme. We need to recognize the main causes of this highway carnage and take action. According to the U.S. Department of Transportation, 25.1 percent of the roadway fatalities involve an age group constituting only 14.5 percent of the driving public. That group is the age range from 15 to 25. Within that group, one half are males. They are three times more likely to be involved in roadway fatalities, meaning that about 7 percent of the males are responsible for more than 16 percent of roadway fatalities. This proposal may be a hard sell for politicians, but it is time for us to step forward boldly and raise the legal driving age for males nationally to 25, with exceptions only for those in the military and those in emergency positions, such as fire fighting and law enforcement. Some may protest that it is unfair to punish the good young male drivers for the sins of their irresponsible peers. But we're already discriminating by group. Surely we all agree that drivers under a certain age should not be allowed to drive. That age varies from state to state, but it is around 15. We have concluded that those younger than 15 are too immature. We don't say those under 15 should be treated individually, not even on the basis of gender. Instead, we exclude the offending group. With my proposal, we would simply move the legal age of male drivers to 25, lumping those of similar age and same gender together for the good of society. Some might argue that improved drivers' education programs in our school system, better public transportation, the production of vehicles that

---

*All statistics in this article are from the U.S. Bureau of Transportation Statistics: www.bts.gov.

are no more powerful and threatening than they need be, a reduced speed limit, counseling and restrictions for repeat offenders, and a stricter enforcement of existing laws represent a wiser approach to our national problem. However, because those ideas have failed to resonate, and young males have continued to put the pedal to the metal in a flood of blood, it is time for a simple statement that will fit on your bumper sticker:

Guys Shouldn't Drive Till 25

Exercise 4 Discussion and Critical Thinking

1. Underline the proposition, and underline and label the subject and focus parts.

2. How is the proposition introduced (history, testimony, statistics, question)?

3. How does Gallagher qualify (limit) her proposition? Copy the last part of the sentence that states the qualifications.

4. Would this law create some problems not discussed by the author? If so, what kind?

5. Which parts of the argument would you disagree with, and why?

6. Do you think the author is entirely serious about this argument? What author comments might suggest that she is not?

7. Does it make any difference that the author is female? Why or why not?

～ Topics for Paragraphs of Argument

Most of these topics can also be used for short essays.

Reading-Based Writing Topics

See Chapter 5 for instruction and examples for writing summaries, reactions, and two-part responses (separate paragraphs of summary and reaction). Use quotations and references. Credit source(s).

"My Life to Live—or Not"

1. Write an argument in which you agree or disagree with DeSarro. Incorporate your own value system, religious or secular, into your discussion. Use references and quotations.
2. Use the Internet or the library to research the state law in Oregon that permits doctors to assist in suicides under certain conditions. Discuss how well the law has worked and whether it should be enacted as a national law or a law in other states.

"Chick–O–Stick Forever!"

3. Write a reaction to Bradley's paragraph. Refer directly to his ideas and use quotations as you evaluate his assertions. Evaluate his writing for the effectiveness of his persuasiveness. Consider comparing his candy choice with one of your own. (Chick–O–Stick can be found in small markets and in some big box stores such as Wal-Mart and often in convenience stores.)

"A Modest Proposal: Guys Shouldn't Drive Till 25"

4. Write an argument in which you either agree or disagree with Gallagher's views. Refer to and quote from her paragraph. Make it a critique of specifically what she said and what you think she means. Consider using examples from your own experience and observations.
5. Write a paragraph or short essay in which you discuss Gallagher's purpose and technique. Is Gallagher serious in what she is saying, or does she exaggerate to make her point? What phrases or ideas suggest her tone? Be specific and document your work. The title is based on a famous work by Jonathan Swift: "A Modest Proposal." You can find a copy on the Internet by keying in "Jonathan Swift" and "A Modest Proposal" on a

search engine such as Google. Explain how being familiar with Swift's essay helps you understand Gallagher's message.

General Topic

6. Write a paragraph on one of the following broad subject areas. You will have to limit your focus for a paragraph of argument. You may also modify the topics to fit specific situations.

   a. Banning pit bulls, or the breeding of pit bulls
   b. A product that is outstanding as compared with products in the same category. See "Chick–O–Stick Forever!" on page 175 as an example of a paragraph on a similar topic.
   c. School dress codes
   d. Sex education
   e. Sexual harassment
   f. Advertising tobacco
   g. Zone changes for stores selling liquor
   h. Curfew for teenagers
   i. Laws keeping known gang members out of parks

Cross-Curricular Topic

7. From a class you are taking or have taken, or from your major area of study, select an issue on which thoughtful people may disagree and write a paragraph of persuasion or argument. It could be an interpretation of an ambiguous piece of literature for an English class; a position on global warming, public land management, or the Endangered Species Act for a class in ecology; a paper arguing about the effectiveness of government regulation in a political-science class; a view on a certain kind of diet in a food-science class; a preference for a particular worldview in a class on philosophy; or an assertion on the proper role of chiropractors as health-care practitioners in a health-science class.

Career-Related Topic

8. Write a persuasive paragraph in which you argue to solve a problem pertaining to one of the following workplace issues:

   a. Labor unions: strikes, recruiting, open shop, closed shop, right-to-work states
   b. Doing your job (or part of it) at home rather than at the workplace

c. Fringe benefits: health care, vacations, severance pay
d. Evaluation procedures
e. Staggering lunch hours and work breaks
f. Outsourcing jobs

Writer's Guidelines at a Glance: Argument

1. Consider which aspects of the formal argument you need for your paragraph:

   - **Background:** What is the historical or social context for this controversial issue?
   - **Proposition** (the **topic sentence**): What do I want my audience to believe or to do?
   - **Qualification of proposition:** Have I limited my proposition so that those who disagree with me cannot easily challenge me with exceptions?
   - **Refutation** (taking the opposing view into account, mainly to point out its fundamental weakness): What is the view on the other side, and why is it flawed in reasoning or evidence?
   - **Support:** In addition to sound reasoning, have I used appropriate facts, examples, statistics, and opinions of authorities?

2. The basic pattern of a paragraph of argument is likely to be in this form:

   Proposition (the topic sentence)
   I. Support 1
   II. Support 2
   III. Support 3

3. Consider using the Brandon Writing Process Worksheet with the Brandon Guide for Revising and Editing (see the form that can be enlarged and copied from inside the front of this book). Then, after your assignment is returned, update the Self-Evaluation Chart on the back of the front cover.

16

Handbook

This Handbook presents rules, discussion, and examples for grammar, usage, punctuation, capitalization, and spelling. Dealing mainly with fundamentals, it covers elements in the Brandon Guide and explains how to correct all forty-eight common problems listed in the Correction Chart inside the back cover. Page A-1, the Contents pages, the Student Overview, the Index, and this Handbook provide the location of instructions that will guide you in your quest for the writing of paragraphs and short essays that are revised and edited until they are effective and correct.

～ Locating Subjects and Verbs

The **subject** is what the sentence is about, and the **verb** indicates what the subject is doing or is being.

Subjects

You can recognize the **simple subject** by asking *Who?* or *What?* causes the action or expresses the state of being found in the verb.

1. The simple subject and the simple verb can be single or compound.

   My *friend* and *I* have much in common.
   My friend *came* and *left* a present.

2. Although the subject usually appears before the verb, it may follow the verb.

   From tiny acorns grow mighty *oaks.*

3. The **command**, or **imperative**, **sentence** has a "you" as the implied subject, and no stated subject.

   (You) Read the notes.

4. Be careful not to confuse a subject with an object of a preposition.

   The *foreman* [subject] of the *jury* [object of the preposition] directs discussion.

182

Verbs

Verbs show action or express being in relation to the subject of a sentence.

1. **Action verbs** show movement or accomplishment of an idea or a deed.

   He *dropped* the book. (movement)

   He *read* the book. (accomplishment)

2. ***Being*** **verbs** indicate existence.

   They *were* concerned.

3. Verbs may appear as single words or as phrases.

   He *led* the charge. (single word)

   She *is leading* the charge. (phrase)

4. Verbs that are joined by a coordinating conjunction such as *and* and *or* are called **compound verbs**.

   She *worked* for twenty-five years and *retired*.

5. Do not confuse verbs with **verbals**, verblike words that function as other parts of speech.

   The bird *singing* [participle acting as an adjective] in the tree is defending its territory.

   Singing [gerund acting as a noun subject] is fun.

   I want *to eat* [infinitive acting as a noun object].

6. Do not confuse **adverbs** such as *never*, *not*, and *hardly* with verbs; they only modify verbs.

7. Do not overlook a part of the verb that is separated from another in a question.

   Where *had* the defendant *gone* on that fateful night?

⌒ Writing Different Kinds of Sentences

On the basis of number and kinds of clauses, sentences may be classified as simple, compound, complex, and compound-complex.

Clauses

1. A **clause** is a group of words with a subject and a verb that functions as a part or all of a complete sentence. There are two kinds of clauses: independent (main) and dependent (subordinate).

2. An **independent (main) clause** is a group of words with a subject and a verb that can stand alone and make sense. An independent clause expresses a complete thought by itself and can be written as a separate sentence.

    I have the money.

3. A **dependent clause** is a group of words with a subject and a verb that depends on a main clause to give it meaning. The dependent clause functions in the common sentence patterns as a noun, an adjective, or an adverb.

    When I have the money

Kinds of Sentences Defined

Kind	Definition	Example
1. Simple	One independent clause	She did the work well.
2. Compound	Two or more independent clauses (underlined)	She did the work well, and she was paid well.
3. Complex	One independent clause (underlined) and one or more dependent clauses (italicized)	*Because she did the work well*, she was paid well.
4. Compound Complex	Two or more independent clauses and one or more dependent clauses	*Because she did the work well*, she was paid well, and she was satisfied.

Punctuation

1. Use a comma before a coordinating conjunction (*for*, *and*, *nor*, *but*, *or*, *yet*, *so*) between two independent clauses.

    The movie was good, *but* the tickets were expensive.

2. Use a comma after a dependent clause (beginning with a subordinating conjunction such as *because*, *although*, *when*, *since*, or *before*) that occurs before the main clause.

When the bus arrived, we quickly boarded.

3. Use a semicolon between two independent clauses in one sentence if there is no coordinating conjunction.

    The bus arrived; we quickly boarded.

4. Use a semicolon before and usually a comma after a conjunctive adverb (such as *however*, *otherwise*, *therefore*, *on the other hand*, and *in fact*), and between two independent clauses (no comma after *then*, *also*, *now*, *thus*, and *soon*).

    The Dodgers have not played well this year; *however*, the Giants have won ten games in a row.

    Spring training went well; *then* the regular baseball season began.

∼ Combining Sentences

Coordination

If you intend to communicate two equally important and closely related ideas, you certainly will want to place them close together, probably in a **compound sentence** (two or more independent clauses).

1. When you combine two sentences by using a coordinating conjunction, drop the period, change the capital letter to a small letter, and insert a comma before the coordinating conjunction.

    He likes your home. He can visit for only three months.

    He likes your home, *but* he can visit for only three months.

2. When you combine two sentences by using a semicolon, replace the period with a semicolon and change the capital letter that begins the second sentence to a small letter. If you wish to use a conjunctive adverb, insert it after the semicolon and usually put a comma after it.

    He likes your home; he can visit for only three months.

    He likes your home; *however*, he can visit for only three months.

Subordination

If you have two ideas that are closely related but one is secondary to or dependent on the other, you may want to use a complex sentence.

My neighbors are considerate. They never play loud music.

Because my neighbors are considerate, they never play loud music.

1. If the dependent clause comes *before* the main clause, set it off with a comma.

   Before you dive, be sure there is water in the pool.

2. If the dependent clause comes *after* or *within* the main clause, set it off with a comma only if you use the word *though* or *although* or if the words are not necessary to convey the basic meaning in the sentence.

   Be sure there is water in the pool *before you dive.*

Coordination and Subordination

At times you may want to show the relationship of three or more ideas within one sentence. If that relationship involves two or more main ideas and one or more supporting ideas, the combination can be stated in a **compound-complex sentence** (two or more independent clauses and one or more dependent clauses).

Before he learned how to operate a computer, he had trouble

dependent clause

with his typewritten assignments, but now he produces clean,

independent clause   independent clause

attractive material.

Use punctuation consistent with that of the compound and complex sentences.

Other Methods of Combining Ideas

1. Simple sentences can often be combined by using a **prepositional phrase**, a preposition followed by a noun or pronoun object.

   Dolly Parton wrote a song about a coat. The coat had many colors.

   Dolly Parton wrote a song about a coat *of many colors.*

2. To combine simple sentences, use an **appositive**, a noun phrase that immediately follows a noun or pronoun and renames it.

   Susan is the leading scorer on the team. Susan is a quick and strong player.

   Susan, *a quick and strong player*, is the leading scorer on the team.

3. Simple sentences can often be combined by dropping a repeated subject in the second sentence.

> Some items are too damaged for recycling. They must be disposed of.

> Some items are too damaged for recycling and must be disposed of.

4. Sentences can be combined by using a **participial phrase**, a group of words that include a participle, which is a verblike word that usually ends in *-ing* or *-ed*.

> John rowed smoothly. He reached the shore.

> *Rowing smoothly*, John reached the shore.

～ Variety in Sentences: Types, Order, Length, Beginnings

Do not bother to look for formulas in this section. Variety in sentences may be desirable for its own sake, to avoid dullness. However, it is more likely you will revise your paragraphs for reasons that make good sense in the context of what you are writing. The following are some of the variations available to you.

Types

You have learned that all four types of sentences are sound. Your task as a writer is to decide which one to use for a particular thought. That decision may not be made until you revise your composition. Then you can choose on the basis of the relationship of ideas:

> **Simple:** a single idea
> **Compound:** two closely related ideas
> **Complex:** one idea more important than the other
> **Compound-Complex:** a combination of compound
> and complex ideas

These types of sentences were all covered in more detail earlier in this chapter (page 184).

Order

You will choose the order of parts and information according to what you want to emphasize. Typically the most emphatic location is at the end of any unit.

Length

Uncluttered and direct, short sentences commonly draw attention. Because that focus occurs only when they stand out from longer sentences, however, you would usually avoid a series of short sentences.

Beginnings

A long series of sentences with each beginning containing a subject followed by a verb may become monotonous. Consider beginning sentences in different ways:

> **With a prepositional phrase:** *In the distance* a dog barked.
> **With a transitional connective (conjunctive adverb) such as** *then*, *however*, or *therefore*: *Then* the game was over.
> **With a coordinating conjunction such as** *and* or *but*: *But* no one moved for three minutes.
> **With a dependent clause:** *Although he wanted a new Corvette,* he settled for a used Ford Taurus.
> **With an adverb:** *Carefully* he removed the thorn from the lion's paw.

∼ Correcting Fragments, Comma Splices, and Run-Ons

Fragments

A correct sentence signals completeness. Each complete sentence must have an **independent clause**, meaning a word or a group of words that contains a subject and a verb that can stand alone.

> *He enrolled* for the fall semester.

A **fragment** (a group of words without a subject, without a verb, or without both) signals incompleteness—it doesn't make sense. You would expect the speaker or writer of a fragment to say or write more or to rephrase it.

1. A **dependent clause**, which begins with a subordinating word, cannot stand by itself.

> *Because* he left.
>
> *When* she worked.
>
> *Although* they slept.

2. A **verbal phrase**, a **prepositional phrase**, and an **appositive phrase** may carry ideas, but each is incomplete because it lacks a subject and a verb.

Verbal phrase	*having studied hard all evening*
Sentence	Having studied hard all evening, John decided to retire.
Prepositional phrase	*in the store*
Sentence	She worked in the store.
Appositive phrase	*a successful business*
Sentence	Marks Brothers, a successful business, sells clothing.

Comma Splices and Run-Ons

The **comma splice** consists of two independent clauses with only a comma between them.

> *The weather was disappointing,* <u>we canceled the picnic.</u>

A comma by itself cannot join two independent clauses.

The **run-on** differs from the comma splice in only one respect: It has no comma between the independent clauses. Therefore, the run-on is two independent clauses with *nothing* between them.

> *The weather was disappointing* <u>we canceled the picnic.</u>

Independent clauses must be properly connected.

Correct comma splices and run-ons by using a comma and a coordinating conjunction, a subordinating conjunction, or a semicolon, or by making each clause a separate sentence.

1. Use a comma and a **coordinating conjunction** (*for, and, nor, but, or, yet, so*).

   We canceled the picnic, *for* the weather was disappointing.

2. Use a **subordinating conjunction** (such as *because, after, that, when, although, since, how, until, unless, before*) to make one clause dependent.

   Because the weather was disappointing, we canceled the picnic.

3. Use a **semicolon** (with or without a conjunctive adverb such as *however, otherwise, therefore, similarly, hence, on the other hand, then, consequently, also, thus*).

The weather was disappointing; we canceled the picnic.

The weather was disappointing; *therefore,* we canceled the picnic.

4. Make each clause a separate sentence. For a comma splice, replace the comma with a period, and begin the second sentence (clause) with a capital letter. For a run-on, insert a period between the two independent clauses and begin the second sentence with a capital letter.

The weather was disappointing. We canceled the picnic.

∼ Omissions: When Parts Are Missing

Do not omit words that are needed to make your sentences clear and logical. Of the many types of undesirable constructions in which necessary words are omitted, the following are the most common.

1. **Subjects.** Do not omit a necessary subject in a sentence with two verbs.

    ILLOGICAL   The cost of the car was $12,000 but would easily last me through college. (subject of *last*)

    LOGICAL   The cost of the car was $12,000, but the car would easily last me through college.

2. **Verbs.** Do not omit verbs that are needed because of a change in the number of the subject or a change of tense.

    ILLOGICAL   The bushes were trimmed and the grass mowed.

    LOGICAL   The bushes were trimmed, and the grass was mowed.

    ILLOGICAL   True honesty always has and always will be admired by most people. (tense)

    LOGICAL   True honesty always has been and always will be admired by most people.

3. ***That* as a conjunction.** The conjunction *that* should not be omitted from a dependent clause if there is danger of misreading the sentence.

    MISLEADING   We believed Eric, if not stopped, would hurt himself.

    CLEAR   We believed that Eric, if not stopped, would hurt himself.

4. **Prepositions.** Do not omit prepositions in idiomatic phrases, in expressions of time, and in parallel phrases.

ILLOGICAL   Weekends the campus is deserted. (time)
LOGICAL   During weekends the campus is deserted.

ILLOGICAL   I have neither love nor patience with untrained dogs. (parallel phrases)
LOGICAL   I have neither love for nor patience with untrained dogs.

ILLOGICAL   Glenda's illness was something we heard only after her recovery.
LOGICAL   Glenda's illness was something we heard about only after her recovery.

Working with Verb Forms

The twelve verb tenses are shown in this section. The irregular verb *drive* is used as the example. (See pages 193–195 for a list of irregular verbs.)

Simple Tenses

Present
I, we, you, they *drive.*   May imply
He, she, it *drives.*   a continuation from
                                        past to future

Past
I, we, you, he, she, it, they *drove.*

Future
I, we, you, he, she, it, they *will drive.*

Perfect Tenses

Present Perfect
I, we, you, they *have driven.*   Completed recently
He, she, it *has driven.*   in the past, may continue
                                        to the present

Past Perfect
I, we, you, he, she, it, they   Completed prior to a
had driven.   specific time in the past

Future Perfect

I, we, you, he, she, it, they
will have driven.

Will occur at a time
prior to a specific
time in the future

Progressive Tenses

Present Progressive

I *am driving.*
He, she, it *is driving.*
We, you, they *are driving.*

In progress now

Past Progressive

I, he, she, it *was driving.*
We, you, they *were driving.*

In progress in the
past

Future Progressive

I, we, you, he, she, it, they
will be driving.

In progress in the
future

Perfect Progressive Tenses

Present Perfect Progressive

I, we, you, they *have been driving.*
He, she, it *has been driving.*

In progress up to now

Past Perfect Progressive

I, we, you, he, she, it, they *had
been driving.*

In progress before
another event in the past

Future Perfect Progressive

I, we, you, he, she, it, they *will
have been driving.*

In progress before
another event in the future

Past Participles

The past participle uses the helping verbs *has, have,* or *had* along with
the past tense of the verb. For regular verbs, whose past tense ends in
-ed, the past participle form of the verb is the same as the past tense.

Following is a list of some common regular verbs, showing the
base form, the past tense, and the past participle. (The base form can
also be used with such helping verbs as *can, could, do, does, did,
may, might, must, shall, should, will,* and *would.*)

Regular Verbs

Base Form (Present)	Past	Past Participle
ask	asked	asked
answer	answered	answered

Base Form (Present)	Past	Past Participle
cry	cried	cried
decide	decided	decided
dive	dived (dove)	dived
drag	dragged	dragged
finish	finished	finished
happen	happened	happened
learn	learned	learned
like	liked	liked
love	loved	loved
need	needed	needed
open	opened	opened
start	started	started
suppose	supposed	supposed
walk	walked	walked
want	wanted	wanted

Whereas **regular verbs** are predictable—having an *-ed* ending for past and past participle forms—**irregular verbs**, as the term suggests, follow no definite pattern.

Following is a list of some common irregular verbs, showing the base form (present), the past tense, and the past participle.

Irregular Verbs

Base Form (Present)	Past	Past Participle
arise	arose	arisen
awake	awoke (awaked)	awaked
be	was, were	been
become	became	become
begin	began	begun
bend	bent	bent
blow	blew	blown
break	broke	broken
bring	brought	brought
buy	bought	bought
catch	caught	caught
choose	chose	chosen
cling	clung	clung
come	came	come
creep	crept	crept

Base Form (Present)	Past	Past Participle
deal	dealt	dealt
do	did	done
drink	drank	drunk
drive	drove	driven
eat	ate	eaten
feel	felt	felt
fight	fought	fought
fling	flung	flung
fly	flew	flown
forget	forgot	forgotten
freeze	froze	frozen
get	got	got (gotten)
go	went	gone
grow	grew	grown
have	had	had
know	knew	known
lead	led	led
leave	left	left
lose	lost	lost
mean	meant	meant
read	read	read
ride	rode	ridden
ring	rang	rung
see	saw	seen
shine	shone	shone
shoot	shot	shot
sing	sang	sung
sink	sank	sunk
sleep	slept	slept
slink	slunk	slunk
speak	spoke	spoken
spend	spent	spent
steal	stole	stolen
stink	stank (stunk)	stunk
sweep	swept	swept
swim	swam	swum
swing	swung	swung
take	took	taken
teach	taught	taught
tear	tore	torn

Base Form (Present)	Past	Past Participle
think	thought	thought
throw	threw	thrown
wake	woke (waked)	woken (waked)
weep	wept	wept
write	wrote	written

"Problem" Verbs

The following pairs of verbs are especially troublesome and confusing: *lie* and *lay*, *sit* and *set*, and *rise* and *raise*. One way to tell them apart is to remember which word in each pair takes a direct object. A direct object answers the question *whom* or *what* in connection with a verb. The words *lay*, *raise*, and *set* take a direct object.

> He *raised* the window. (He *raised* what?)

Lie, *rise*, and *sit*, however, cannot take a direct object. We cannot say, for example, "He rose the window." In the following examples, the italicized words are objects.

Present Tense	Meaning	Past Tense	Past Participle	Example
lie	to rest	lay	lain	I lay down to rest.
lay	to place something	laid	laid	We laid the *books* on the table.
rise	to go up	rose	risen	The smoke rose quickly.
raise	to lift	raised	raised	She raised the *question.*
sit	to rest	sat	sat	He sat in the chair.
set	to place something	set	set	They set the *basket* on the floor.

Verb Tense

Verb tense is a word form indicating time. The rules about selecting a **tense** for certain kinds of writing are flexible. You should be consistent, however, changing tense only for a good reason.

Usually you should select the present tense to write about literature.

Moby Dick *is* a famous white whale.

Select the past tense to write about yourself (usually) or something historical (always).

I *was* eighteen when I *decided* I *was* ready for independence.

Subject-Verb Agreement

The basic principle of **subject-verb agreement** is that if the subject is singular, the verb should be singular, and if the subject is plural, the verb should be plural. There are ten major guidelines. In the examples under the following guidelines, the true subjects and verbs are italicized.

1. Do not let words that come between the subject and verb affect agreement.

   a. Modifying phrases and clauses frequently come between the subject and verb:

      The various *types* of drama *were* not *discussed*.

      Angela, who is hitting third, *is* the best player.

      The *price* of those shoes *is* too high.

   b. Certain prepositions can cause trouble. The following words are prepositions, not conjunctions: *along with*, *as well as*, *besides*, *in addition to*, *including*, and *together with*. The words that function as objects of prepositions cannot also be subjects of the sentence.

      The *coach*, along with the players, *protests* the decision.

   c. In compound subjects in which one subject is positive and one subject is negative, the verb agrees with the positive subject.

      Phillip, not the other boys, *was* the culprit.

2. Do not let inversions (verb before subject, not the normal order) affect the agreement of subject and verb.

   a. Verbs and other words may come before the subject. Do not let them affect the agreement. To understand subject-verb relationships, recast the sentence in normal word order.

      Are Juan and his *sister* at home? (question form)

      Juan and his *sister are* at home. (normal order)

   b. A sentence filler is a word that is grammatically independent of other words in the sentence. The most common fillers are *there* and *here*. Even though a sentence filler precedes the verb, it should not be treated as the subject.

> There *are* many *reasons* for his poor work. (The verb *are* agrees with the subject *reasons*.)

3. A singular verb agrees with a singular indefinite pronoun.

   a. Most indefinite pronouns are singular.

   > *Each* of the women *is* ready at this time.
   >
   > *Neither* of the women *is* ready at this time.
   >
   > *One* of the children *is* not paying attention.

   b. Certain indefinite pronouns do not clearly express either a singular or plural number. Agreement, therefore, depends on the meaning of the sentence. These pronouns are *all*, *any*, *none*, and *some*.

   > *All* of the melon *was* good.
   >
   > *All* of the melons *were* good.
   >
   > *None* of the pie *is* acceptable.
   >
   > *None* of the pies *are* acceptable.

4. Two or more subjects joined by *and* usually take a plural verb.

   > The *captain* and the *sailors were* happy to be ashore.
   >
   > The *trees* and *shrubs need* more care.

   a. If the parts of a compound subject mean one and the same person or thing, the verb is singular; if the parts mean more than one, the verb is plural.

   > The *secretary* and *treasurer is* not present. (one person)
   >
   > The *secretary* and the *treasurer are* not present. (more than one person)

   b. When *each* or *every* modify singular subjects joined by *and*, the verb is singular.

   > Each *boy* and each *girl brings* a donation.
   >
   > Every *woman* and *man has asked* the same questions.

5. Alternative subjects—that is, subjects joined by *or, nor, either/ or, neither/nor, not only/but also*—should be handled in the following manner.

   a. If the subjects are both singular, the verb is singular.

Rosa or *Alicia* is responsible.

b. If the subjects are plural, the verb is plural.

Neither the *students* nor the *teachers were* impressed by his comments.

c. If one of the subjects is singular and the other subject is plural, the verb agrees with the nearer subject.

Either the Garcia *boys* or their *father goes* to the hospital each day.

Either their *father* or the Garcia *boys go* to the hospital each day.

6. Collective nouns—*team, family, group, crew, gang, class, faculty*, and the like—take a singular verb if the verb is considered a unit, but a plural verb if the group is considered as a number of individuals.

The *team is playing* well tonight.

The *team are getting* dressed. (Here the individuals are acting not as a unit but separately. If you don't like the way this sounds, rewrite as "The members of the team are getting dressed.")

7. Titles of books, essays, short stories, and plays, a word spoken of as a word, and the names of businesses take a singular verb.

The Canterbury Tales was written by Geoffrey Chaucer.

Markle Brothers has a sale this week.

8. Sums of money, distances, and measurements are followed by a singular verb when a unit is meant. They are followed by a plural verb when the individual elements are considered separately.

Three dollars was the price. (unit)

Three dollars were lying there. (individual)

Five years is a long time. (unit)

The *first five years were* difficult ones. (individual)

9. Be careful of agreement with nouns ending in -s. Several nouns ending in -s take a singular verb—for example, *aeronautics, civics, economics, ethics, measles*, and *mumps*.

Mumps is an extremely unpleasant disease.

Economics is my major field of study.

10. Some nouns have only a plural form and so take only a plural verb—for example, *clothes, fireworks, scissors*, and *pants*.

His *pants are* badly wrinkled.

Mary's *clothes were* stylish and expensive.

⁓ Giving Verbs Voice

Which of these sentences sounds better to you?

Miguel Cabrera slammed a home run.

A home run was slammed by Miguel Cabrera.

Both sentences carry the same message, but the first expresses it more effectively. The subject (*Miguel Cabrera*) is the actor. The verb (*slammed*) is the action. The direct object (*home run*) is the receiver of the action. The second sentence lacks the vitality of the first because the receiver of the action is the subject; the doer is embedded in the prepositional phrase at the end of the sentence.

The first sentence demonstrates the active voice. It has an active verb (one that leads to a direct object), and the action moves from the beginning to the end of the sentence. The second exhibits the passive voice (with the action reflecting back on the subject). When given a choice, you should usually select the active voice. It promotes energy and directness.

The passive voice, though not usually the preferred form, does have its uses:

- When the doer of the action is unknown or unimportant

  My car was stolen. (The doer, a thief, is unknown.)

- When the receiver of the action is more important than the doer

  My neighbor was permanently disabled by an irresponsible drunk driver. (The neighbor's suffering, not the drunk driver, is the focus.)

As you can see, the passive construction places the doer at the end of a prepositional phrase (as in the second example) or does not include the doer in the statement at all (as in the first example). The passive voice places the receiver of the action in the subject position, and it presents the verb in its past tense form preceded by a *to be* helper. The transformation is a simple one:

ACTIVE   She read the book.

PASSIVE   The book was read by her.

Because weak sentences often involve the unnecessary and ineffective use of the passive form, you should learn to identify passive
constructions and consider changing them to active.

⌒ Selecting Pronoun Case

A **pronoun** is a word that is used in place of a noun. **Case** is the form
a pronoun takes as it fills a position in a sentence.

1. **Subjective pronouns** are *I*, *he*, and *she* (singular), and *we* and
   they (plural). *Who* can be either singular or plural. Subjective-
   case pronouns can fill subject positions in a sentence.

   We dance in the park.

   It was *she* who spoke. (referring back to and meaning the same
   as the subject)

2. **Objective pronouns** are *me*, *him*, and *her* (singular); and *us* and
   them (plural). *Whom* can be either singular or plural. Objective-
   case pronouns fill object positions.

   We saw *her* in the library. (object of verb)

   They gave the results to *us*—Judy and *me*. (object of a preposition)

3. Three techniques are useful for deciding what pronoun case to use.

   a. If you have a compound element (such as a subject or an ob-
      ject of a preposition), consider only the pronoun part.

      They will visit Jim and (I, me). (*Consider:* They will visit *me*.)

   b. If the next important word after *who* or *whom* in a state-
      ment is a noun or pronoun, the word choice will be *whom*;
      otherwise, it will be *who*. Disregard qualifier clauses such as
      It seems and *I feel*.

      The person *who* works hardest will win.

      The person *whom* judges like will win.

      The person *who*, we think, worked hardest won. (ignoring the
      qualifier clause)

   c. *Let's* is made up of the words *let* and *us* and means *"you let
      us"*; therefore, when you select a pronoun to follow it, consider
      the two original words and select another object word—*me*.

      Let's you and *me* go to town.

∿ Matching Pronouns and Antecedents

A pronoun agrees with its antecedent in person, number, and gender.

1. Avoid needless shifting in **person**, which means shifting in point of view, such as from *I* to *you*.

   > INCORRECT   *I* tried but *you* couldn't persuade her to return.

   > CORRECT   *I* tried but *I* couldn't persuade her to return.

2. Most problems with pronoun-antecedent agreement involve number. The principles are simple: If the antecedent (the word the pronoun refers back to) is singular, use a singular pronoun. If the antecedent is plural, use a plural pronoun.

   > Jim forgot *his* notebook.

   > Many students cast *their* votes today.

   > Someone lost *his* or *her* [not *their*] book.

3. The pronoun should agree with its antecedent in gender, if the gender of the antecedent is specific. Masculine and feminine pronouns are gender-specific: *he, him, she,* and *her.* Others are neuter: *I, we, me, us, it, they, them, who, whom, that,* and *which.* The words *who* and *whom* refer to people. *That* can refer to ideas, things, and people, but usually not to people. *Which* refers to ideas and things but never to people. To avoid a perceived sex bias, most writers and speakers prefer to use *he or she* or *his or her* instead of just *he* or *his*; however, many writers simply make antecedents plural.

   > Everyone should work until *he or she* drops.

   > People should work until *they* drop.

∿ Using Adjectives and Adverbs

1. **Adjectives** modify (describe) nouns and pronouns and answer the questions *Which one? What kind?* and *How many?*
2. **Adverbs** modify verbs, adjectives, or other adverbs and answer the questions *How? Where? When?* and *To what degree?* Most words ending in *-ly* are adverbs.
3. If you settle for a common word such as *good* or a slang word such as *neat* to characterize something you like, you will be limiting your communication. The more precise the word, the

better the communication. Keep in mind, however, that anything can be overdone; therefore, use adjectives and adverbs
wisely and economically.

4. For making comparisons, most adjectives and adverbs have
   three different forms: the positive (one), the comparative (two),
   and the superlative (three or more).

   a. Adjectives

      ■ Add -*er* to short adjectives (one or two syllables) to rank
        units of two.

        Julian is *kinder* than Sam.

      ■ Add -*est* to short adjectives (one or two syllables) to rank
        units of more than two.

        Of the fifty people I know, Julian is the *kindest.*

      ■ Add the word *more* before long adjectives to rank units of
        two.

        My hometown is *more beautiful* than yours.

      ■ Add the word *most* before long adjectives to rank units of
        three or more.

        My hometown is the *most beautiful* in all America.

      ■ Some adjectives are irregular in the way they change to
        show comparison: *good, better, best; bad, worse, worst.*

   b. Adverbs

      For most adverbs, use the word *more* before the comparative
      form (two) and the word *most* before the superlative form (three
      or more).

      Jim performed *skillfully.* (modifier)

      Joan performed *more skillfully* than Morton. (comparative
      modifier)

      But Susan performed *most skillfully* of all. (superlative modifier)

5. Avoid double negatives. Words such as *no, not, none, nothing,
   never, hardly, barely,* and *scarcely* should not be combined.

   INCORRECT   I *don't* have *no* time for recreation.

   CORRECT   I have *no* time for recreation.

   CORRECT   I *don't* have time for recreation.

6. Do not confuse adjectives (*bad*) with adverbs (*badly*).

    INCORRECT   I feel *badly* about being late.
      CORRECT   I feel *bad* about being late.

    INCORRECT   He handled the situation *bad*.
      CORRECT   He handled the situation *badly*.

∼ Eliminating Dangling and Misplaced Modifiers

1. A modifier that gives information but doesn't refer to a word or group of words already in the sentence is called a **dangling modifier**.

    DANGLING   *Walking down the street*, a snake startled me.

    CORRECT   *Walking down the street*, I was startled by a snake.

2. A modifier that is placed so that it modifies the wrong word or words is called a **misplaced modifier**.

    MISPLACED   The sick man went to a doctor *with a high fever*.

    CORRECT   The sick man with a high fever went to a doctor.

∼ Balancing Sentence Parts

1. **Parallelism** means balancing one structure with another of the same kind—nouns with nouns, verbs with verbs, adjectives (words that can describe nouns) with adjectives, adverbs (words that can describe verbs) with adverbs, and so forth.

    Men, women, and *children* [nouns] *enjoy* the show and *return* [verbs] each year.

    She fell *in love* and *out of love* [prepositional phrases] in a few seconds.

    She fell in love with him, and *he fell in love with her* [clauses].

2. Faulty parallel structure is awkward and draws unfavorable attention to what is being said.

    To talk with his buddies and *eating* fast foods were his favorite pastimes. (The sentence should be *Talking . . .* and *eating* or *To talk . . .* and *to eat.*)

3. Some words signal parallel structure. All coordinating conjunctions (*for, and, nor, but, or, yet, so*) can give such signals.

The weather is hot *and* humid.

He purchased a Dodger Dog, *but* I chose Stadium Peanuts.

4. Combination words also signal the need for parallelism or balance. The most common combination words are *either/or*, *neither/nor*, *not only/but also*, *both/and*, and *whether/or*.

We will *either* win this game *or* go out fighting. (verb following each of the combination words)

Avoiding Wordy Phrases

Certain phrases clutter sentences, consuming our time in writing and our readers' time in reading. Watch for wordy phrases as you revise and edit.

WORDY   *Due to the fact that* he was unemployed, he had to use public transportation.

CONCISE *Because* he was unemployed, he had to use public transportation.

WORDY   *Deep down inside* he believed that the Red Sox would win.

CONCISE He believed that the Red Sox would win.

Note the differences between *Wordy* and *Concise* phrasing:

Wordy	Concise
at the present time	now
basic essentials	essentials
blend together	blend
it is clear that	(delete)
due to the fact that	because
for the reason that	because
I felt inside	I felt
in most cases	usually
as a matter of fact	in fact
in the event that	if
until such time as	until
I personally feel	I feel
in this modern world	today
in order to	to

Wordy	Concise
most of the people	most people
along the lines of	like
past experience	experience
at that point in time	then
in the final analysis	finally
in the near future	soon
have a need for	need
in this day and age	now

∼ Mastering Punctuation

1. The three marks of end punctuation are periods, question marks, and exclamation points.

   a. Periods

   Place a period after a statement.
   Place a period after common abbreviations.

   Use an ellipsis—three periods within a sentence and four periods at the end of a sentence—to indicate that words have been omitted from quoted material.

   > He stopped walking and the buildings . . . rose up out of the misty courtroom. . . . (James Thurber, "The Secret Life of Walter Mitty")

   b. Question marks

   Place a question mark at the end of a direct question.
   Use a single question mark in sentence constructions that contain a double question—that is, a quoted question within a question.

   > Mr. Martin said, "Did he say, 'Are we going?'"

   Do *not* use a question mark after an indirect (reported) question.

   > She asked me what caused the slide.

   c. Exclamation points

   Place an exclamation point after a word or group of words that expresses strong feeling.
   Do not overwork the exclamation point. Do not use double exclamation points.

2. The comma is used essentially to separate and to set off sentence elements.

   a. Use a comma to separate main clauses joined by one of the coordinating conjunctions—*for, and, nor, but, or, yet, so.*

      We went to the game, *but* it was canceled.

   b. Use a comma after introductory dependent clauses and long introductory phrases (generally, four or more words is considered long).

      Before she and I arrived, the meeting was called to order.

   c. Use a comma to separate words, phrases, and clauses in a series.

      He ran *down the street, across the park,* and *into the arms* of his father.

   d. Use a comma to separate coordinate adjectives not joined by *and* that modify the same noun.

      I need a *sturdy, reliable* truck.

   e. Use a comma to separate sentence elements that might be misread.

      Inside, the dog scratched his fleas.

   f. Use commas to set off (enclose) nonessential (unnecessary for meaning of the sentence) words, phrases, and clauses.

      Maria, *who studied hard*, will pass.

   g. Use commas to set off parenthetical elements such as mild interjections (*oh, well, yes, no,* and others), most conjunctive adverbs (*however, otherwise, therefore, similarly, hence, on the other hand,* and *consequently,* but not *then, thus, soon, now,* and *also*), quotation indicators, and special abbreviations (*etc., i.e., e.g.,* and others).

      Oh, what a silly question! (mild interjection)

      It is necessary, *of course,* to leave now. (sentence modifier)

      We left early; *however,* we missed the train anyway. (conjunctive adverb)

      "When I was in school," *he said,* "I read widely." (quotation indicator)

Books, papers, pens, *etc.*, were scattered on the floor. (The abbreviation *etc.*, however, should be used sparingly.)

h. Use commas to set off nouns used as direct address.

Play it again, *Sam.*

i. Use commas to separate the numbers in a date.

June *4, 1965,* is a day I will remember.

j. Use commas to separate the city from the state. No comma is used between the state and the zip code.

Walnut, CA 91789

k. Use a comma following the salutation and the complementary closing in a letter (but in a business letter, use a colon after the salutation).

Dear John,

Sincerely,

l. Use a comma in numbers to set off groups of three digits. However, omit the comma in dates and in long serial numbers, page numbers, and street numbers.

The total assets were *$2,000,000.*

I was born in *1989.*

3. The semicolon indicates a stronger division than the comma. It is used principally to separate independent clauses within a sentence.

a. Use a semicolon to separate independent clauses not joined by a coordinating conjunction.

You must buy that car today; tomorrow will be too late.

b. Use a semicolon between two independent clauses joined by a conjunctive adverb (such as *however, otherwise, therefore, similarly, hence, on the other hand, then, consequently, accordingly, thus*).

It was very late; *therefore,* I remained at the hotel.

4. Quotation marks bring special attention to words.

a. Quotation marks are used principally to set off direct quotations. A direct quotation consists of material taken from the written work or the direct speech of others; it is set off by double quotation marks. Single quotation marks are used to set off a quotation within a quotation.

> He said, "I don't remember if she said, 'Wait for me.'"

b. Use double quotation marks to set off titles of shorter pieces of writing such as magazine articles, essays, short stories, short poems, one-act plays, chapters in books, songs, and separate pieces of writing published as part of a larger work.

> The book *Literature: Structure, Sound, and Sense* contains a deeply moving poem titled "On Wenlock Edge."

> Have you read "The Use of Force," a short story by William Carlos Williams?

> My favorite Elvis song is "Don't Be Cruel."

c. Punctuation with quotation marks follows definite rules.

- A period or comma is always placed *inside* the quotation marks.

> Our assignment for Monday was to read Poe's "The Raven."

> "I will read you the story," he said. "It is a good one."

- A semicolon or colon is always placed *outside* the quotation marks.

> He read Robert Frost's poem "Design"; then he gave the examination.

- A question mark, an exclamation point, or a dash is placed *outside* the quotation marks when it applies to the entire sentence and *inside* the quotation marks when it applies to the material in quotation marks.

> He asked, "Am I responsible for everything?" (quoted question within a statement)

> Did you hear him say, "I have the answer"? (statement within a question)

> Did she say, "Are we ready?" (question within a question)

> She shouted, "Impossible!" (exclamation)

> "I hope—that is, I—" he began. (dash)

5. Italics (slanting type) is used to call special attention to certain words or groups of words. In handwriting, such words are <u>underlined</u>.

   a. Italicize (underline) foreign words and phrases that are still listed in the dictionary as foreign.

   c'est la vie   Weltschmerz

   b. Italicize (underline) titles of books (except the Bible); long poems; plays; magazines; motion pictures; musical compositions; newspapers; works of art; names of aircraft; ships; and letters, figures, and words referred to by their own name.

   War and Peace   Apollo 12   leaving *o* out of *sophomore*

6. The dash is used when a stronger break than the comma is needed. It can also be used to indicate a break in the flow of thought and to emphasize words (less formal than the colon in this situation).

   Here is the true reason—but maybe you don't care.

   English, French, history—these are the subjects I like.

7. The colon is a formal mark of punctuation used chiefly to introduce something that is to follow, such as a list, a quotation, or an explanation.

   These cars are my favorites: Cadillac, Chevrolet, Buick, Oldsmobile, and Pontiac.

8. Parentheses are used to set off material that is of relatively little importance to the main thought of the sentence. Such material—numbers that designate items in a series, figures, supplementary material, and sometimes explanatory details—merely amplifies the main thought.

   The years of the era (1961–1973) were full of action.

   Her husband (she had been married only a year) died last week.

9. Brackets are used within a quotation to set off editorial additions or corrections made by the person who is quoting.

   Churchill said: "It [the Yalta Agreement] contained many mistakes."

10. The apostrophe is used with nouns and indefinite pronouns to show possession; to show the omission of letters and figures in contractions; and to form the plurals of letters, figures, and words referred to as words.

> man's coat   girls' clothes
>
> you're (contraction of *you are*)   five *and*'s

11. The hyphen brings two or more words together into a single compound word. Correct hyphenation, therefore, is essentially a spelling problem rather than one of punctuation. Because the hyphen is not used with any degree of consistency, consult your dictionary for current usage. Study the following as a beginning guide.

   a. Use a hyphen to separate the parts of many compound words.

   > about-face   go-between

   b. Use a hyphen between prefixes and proper names.

   > all-American   mid-November

   c. Use a hyphen to join two or more words used as a single adjective modifier before a noun.

   > first-class service   hard-fought game
   > sad-looking mother

   d. Use a hyphen with spelled-out compound numbers up to ninety-nine and with fractions.

   > twenty-six   two-thirds

Note: Dates, street addresses, numbers requiring more than two words, chapter and page numbers, time followed directly by *a.m.* or *p.m.*, and figures after a dollar sign or before measurement abbreviations are usually written as figures, not words.

⌒ Conquering Capitalization

In English, there are many conventions concerning the use of capital letters. Here are some of them.

1. Capitalize the first word of a sentence.
2. Capitalize proper nouns and adjectives derived from proper nouns.

   ■ Names of persons
     Edward Jones

- Adjectives derived from proper nouns
    - Shakespearean sonnet   a Miltonic sonnet
- Countries, nationalities, races, and languages
    - Germany   English   Spanish   Chinese
- States, regions, localities, and other geographical divisions
    - California   the Far East   the South
- Oceans, lakes, mountains, deserts, streets, and parks
    - Lake Superior   Sahara Desert   Fifth Avenue
- Educational institutions, schools, and courses
    - Santa Ana College   Joe Hill School
    - Rowland High School   Spanish 3
- Organizations and their members
    - Boston Red Sox   Audubon Society   Boy Scouts
- Corporations, governmental agencies or departments, trade names
    - U.S. Steel Corporation   Treasury Department
    - White Memorial Library   Coke
- Calendar references such as holidays, days of the week, months
    - Easter   Tuesday   January
- Historic eras, periods, documents, laws
    - First Crusade   Romantic Age
    - Declaration of Independence   Geneva Convention

3. Capitalize words denoting family relationships when they are used before a name or substituted for a name.

> He walked with his nephew and Aunt Grace.

> *but*

> He walked with his nephew and his aunt.

> Grandmother and Mother are away on vacation.

> *but*

> My grandmother and my mother are away on vacation.

4. Capitalize abbreviations after names.

> Henry White Jr.   William Green, M.D.

5. Capitalize titles of themes, books, plays, movies, poems, magazines, newspapers, musical compositions, songs, and works

of art. Do not capitalize short conjunctions and prepositions unless they come at the beginning or the end of the title.

Desire Under the Elms	*The Terminator*
The Last of the Mohicans	*Of Mice and Men*
"Blueberry Hill"	

6. Capitalize any title preceding a name or used as a substitute for a name. Do not capitalize a title following a name.

Judge Stone	Alfred Stone, a judge
General Clark	Raymond Clark, a general
Professor Fuentes	Harry Jones, the former president

～ Spelling and Commonly Confused Words

Rules and Tips

- **Do not add letters.**

Incorrect	Correct	Incorrect	Correct
ath*e*lete	athlete	co*m*ming	coming
drown*d*ed	drowned	folk*e*s	folks
occa*s*sionally	occasionally	o*m*mission	omission
pas*t*time	pastime	privile*d*ge	privilege
simil*i*ar	similar	tra*d*gedy	tragedy

- **Do not transpose letters.**

Incorrect	Correct	Incorrect	Correct
alu*nm*i	*alumni*	child*er*n	child*re*n
dup*il*cate	dup*li*cate	irreve*l*ant	irre*l*evant
kind*el*	kind*le*	p*re*haps	p*er*haps
p*er*fer	p*re*fer	p*er*scription	p*re*scription
princip*el*s	princip*le*s	ye*i*ld	y*ie*ld

Note: Whenever you notice other words that fall into any one of these categories, add them to the list.

Except after *c*
Or when sounded as *a*
As in *neighbor* and *weigh*.
i before e

achieve	belief	believe	brief
chief	field	grief	hygiene

niece	piece	pierce	relief
relieve	shield	siege	variety

Except after c

ceiling	conceit	conceive	deceit
deceive	perceive	receipt	receive

Exceptions: either, financier, height, leisure, neither, seize, species, weird

When sounded as a

deign	eight	feign	feint
freight	heinous	heir	neigh
neighbor	rein	reign	skein
sleigh	veil	vein	weigh

- **Apply the rules for dropping the final *e* or retaining the final *e* when a suffix is added.**

  Words ending in a silent *e* usually drop the *e* before a suffix beginning with a vowel; for example, *accuse* + *-ing* = *accusing*. Some common suffixes beginning with a vowel are the following: *-able, -al, -age, -ary, -ation, -ence, -ing, -ion, -ous, -ure.*

admire + *-able* = admirable	arrive + *-al* = arrival
come + *-ing* = coming	explore + *-ation* = exploration
fame + *-ous* = famous	imagine + *-ary* = imaginary
locate + *-ion* = location	please + *-ure* = pleasure
plume + *-age* = plumage	precede + *-ence* = precedence

  Exceptions: dye + -ing = dyeing (to distinguish it from *dying*), acreage, mileage.

  Words ending in a silent *e* usually retain the *e* before a suffix beginning with a consonant; for example: *arrange* + *-ment* = *arrangement*. Some common suffixes beginning with a consonant are the following: *-craft, -ful, -less, -ly, -mate, -ment, -ness, -ty.*

entire + *-ty* = entirety	hate + *-ful* = hateful
hope + *-less* = hopeless	like + *-ness* = likeness
manage + *-ment* = management	safe + *-ly* = safely
stale + *-mate* = stalemate	state + *-craft* = statecraft

  Exceptions: Some words taking the *-ful* or *-ly* suffixes drop the final *e*:

awe + *-ful* = awful	due + *-ly* = duly
true + *-ly* = truly	whole + *-ly* = wholly

Some words taking the suffix -*ment* drop the final *e*; for example:

acknowledgment   argument   judgment

Words ending in silent *e* after *c* or *g* retain the *e* when the suffix begins with the vowel *a* or *o*. The final *e* is retained to keep the *c* or *g* soft before the suffixes.

advantageous   courageous
noticeable   peaceable

- **Apply the rules for doubling a final consonant before a suffix beginning with a vowel.**

Words of one syllable:

blot	blotted	brag	bragging	cut	cutting
drag	dragged	drop	dropped	get	getting
hop	hopper	hot	hottest	man	mannish
plan	planned	rob	robbed	run	running
sit	sitting	stop	stopped	swim	swimming

Words accented on the last syllable:

acquit	acquitted	admit	admittance
allot	allotted	begin	beginning
commit	committee	concur	concurring
confer	conferring	defer	deferring
equip	equipped	occur	occurrence
omit	omitting	prefer	preferred
refer	referred	submit	submitted
transfer	transferred		

Words that are not accented on the last syllable or words that do not end in a single consonant preceded by a vowel do not double the final consonant (regardless of whether the suffix begins with a vowel).

Frequently Misspelled Words

a lot	becoming	development	exaggerate	guard
absence	beginning	difference	excellent	guidance
across	belief	disastrous	exercise	height
actually	benefit	discipline	existence	hoping
all right	buried	discussed	experience	humorous
among	business	disease	explanation	immediately

analyze	certain	divide	extremely	independent
appearance	college	dying	familiar	intelligence
appreciate	coming	eighth	February	interest
argument	committee	eligible	finally	interfere
athlete	competition	Eliminate	foreign	involved
athletics	complete	embarrassed	government	knowledge
awkward	consider	environment	grammar	laboratory
criticism	definitely	especially	grateful	leisure
dependent	develop	etc.	guarantee	length
library	meant	nuclear	particular	possible
likely	medicine	occasionally	persuade	practical
lying	neither	opinion	physically	preferred
marriage	ninety	opportunity	planned	prejudice
mathematics	ninth	parallel	pleasant	privilege
probably	receipt	religious	safety	sense
professor	receive	repetition	scene	separate
prove	recommend	rhythm	schedule	severely
psychology	reference	ridiculous	secretary	shining
pursue	relieve	sacrifice	senior	significant
similar	studying	thoroughly	truly	using
sincerely	succeed	though	unfortunately	usually
sophomore	success	tragedy	unnecessary	Wednesday
speech	suggest	tried	until	writing
straight	surprise	tries	unusual	written

Confused Spelling / Confusing Words

The following are more words that are commonly misspelled or confused with one another. Some have similar sounds, some are often mispronounced, and some are only misunderstood.

a	An article adjective used before a word beginning with a consonant or a consonant sound, as in "I ate *a* donut."
an	An article adjective used before a word beginning with a vowel (*a, e, i, o, u*) or with a silent *h*, as in "I ate *an* artichoke."
and	A coordinating conjunction, as in "Sara *and* I like Johnny Cash."
accept	A verb meaning "to receive," as in "I *accept* your explanation."

except	A preposition meaning "to exclude," as in "I paid everyone *except* you."
advice	A noun meaning "guidance," as in "Thanks for the *advice.*"
advise	A verb meaning "to give guidance," as in "Will you please *advise* me of my rights?"
all right	An adjective meaning "correct" or "acceptable," as in "It's *all right* to cry."
alright	Not used in formal writing.
all ready	An adjective that can be used interchangeably with *ready*, as in "I am *all ready* to go to town."
already	An adverb meaning "before," which cannot be used in place of *ready*, as in "I have *already* finished."
a lot	An adverb meaning "much," as in "She liked him *a lot*," or a noun meaning "several," as in "I had *a lot* of suggestions."
alot	Misspelling.
altogether	An adverb meaning "completely," as in "He is *altogether* happy."
all together	An adverb meaning "as one," which can be used interchangeably with *together*, as in "The group left *all together.*"
could of	Misspelling.
could have	A verb phrase, as in "I *could have* used some kindness."
choose	A present tense verb meaning "to select," as in "Do whatever you *choose.*"
chose	The past tense form of the verb *choose*, as in "They *chose* to take action yesterday."
effect	Usually a noun meaning "result," as in "That *effect* was unexpected."
affect	Usually a verb meaning "change," as in "Ideas *affect* me."
hear	A verb indicating the receiving of sound, as in "I *hear* thunder."
here	An adverb meaning "present location," as in "I live *here.*"
it's	A contraction of *it is*, as in "*It's* time to dance."

its	Possessive pronoun, as in "Each dog has *its* day."
know	A verb usually meaning "to comprehend" or "to recognize," as in "I *know* the answer."
no	An adjective meaning "negative," as in "I have *no* potatoes."
led	The past tense form of the verb *lead*, as in "I *led* a wild life in my youth."
lead	A present tense verb, as in "I *lead* a stable life now" or a noun referring to a substance, such as "I sharpened the *lead* in my pencil."
loose	An adjective meaning "without restraint," as in "He is a *loose* cannon."
lose	A present tense verb from the pattern *lose, lost, lost*, as in "I thought I would *lose* my senses."
paid	The past tense form of *pay*, as in "He *paid* his dues."
payed	Misspelling.
passed	The past tense form of the verb *pass*, meaning "went by," as in "He *passed* me on the curve."
past	An adjective meaning "former," as in "That's *past* history"; or a noun, as in "the *past*."
patience	A noun meaning "willingness to wait," as in "Job was a man of much *patience*."
patients	A noun meaning "people under care," as in "The doctor had fifty *patients*."
peace	A noun meaning "a quality of calmness" or "absence of strife," as in "The guru was at *peace* with the world."
piece	A noun meaning "part," as in "I gave him a *piece* of my mind."
quiet	An adjective meaning "silent," as in "She was a *quiet* child."
quit	A verb meaning "to cease" or "to withdraw," as in "I *quit* my job."
quite	An adverb meaning "very," as in "The clam is *quite* happy."
receive	A verb meaning "to accept," as in "I will *receive* visitors now."

recieve	Misspelling.
stationary	An adjective meaning "not moving," as in "Try to avoid running into *stationary* objects."
stationery	A noun meaning "paper material to write on," as in "I bought a box of *stationery* for Sue's birthday present."
than	A conjunction, as in "He is taller *than* I am."
then	An adverb, as in "She *then* left town."
their	An adjective, as in "They read *their* books."
there	An adverb, as in "He left it *there*," or a filler word as in "*There* is no time left."
they're	A contraction of *they are*, as in "*They're* happy."
to	A preposition, as in "I went *to* town."
too	An adverb meaning "having exceeded or gone beyond what is acceptable," as in "You are *too* late to qualify for the discount," or "also," as in "I have feelings, *too*."
two	An adjective of number, as in "I have *two* jobs."
thorough	An adjective, as in "He did a *thorough* job."
through	A preposition, as in "She went *through* the yard."
truly	An adverb meaning "sincerely" or "completely," as in "He was *truly* happy."
truely	Misspelling.
weather	A noun meaning "condition of the atmosphere," as in "The *weather* is pleasant today."
whether	A conjunction, as in "*Whether* he would go was of no consequence."
write	A present tense verb, as in "Watch me as I *write* this letter."
writen	Misspelling.
written	A past participle verb, as in "I have *written* the letter."
you're	A contraction of *you are*, as in "*You're* my friend."
your	A possessive pronoun, as in "I like *your* looks."

Index

219